INTELLIGENT
TECHNOLOGIES
in Library and Information
Service Applications

F.W. Lancaster
and
Amy Warner

**American Society for
Information Science
and Technology**

ASIST Monograph Series

Published for the
American Society for Information Science and Technology by

 **Information Today, Inc.
Medford, New Jersey**

First printing, April 2001

Intelligent Technologies in Library and Information Service Applications

Library of Congress Cataloging-in-Publication Data

Lancaster, F. Wilfrid (Frederick Wilfrid), 1933-
    Intelligent technologies in library and information service applications /
F.W. Lancaster and Amy
   Warner.
        p. cm. – (ASIST monograph series)
     Includes bibliographical references (p.) and index.
     ISBN 1-57387-103-6
Libraries—Automation. 2. Artificial intelligence—Library applications. 3.
Libraries—Data Processing. 4. Library information networks. 5. Digital
libraries. 6. Libraries—Special collections—Electronic information
resources. I. Warner, Amy J. II. American Society for Information Science
and Technology. III. Title. IV. Series.

Z678.9 .L257 2001
025'.00285—dc21

                                                        00-053951

Publisher: Thomas H. Hogan, Sr.
Editor-in-Chief: John B. Bryans
Managing Editor: Janet M. Spavlik
Copy Editor: John Eichorn
Production Manager: M. Heide Dengler
Cover Designer: Jacqueline Walter
Book Designer: Jeremy Pellegrin

Table of Contents

List of Figures

Preface

The study presented in this book is based primarily on research conducted with the support of the Special Libraries Association's (SLA) Steven I. Goldspiel Memorial Research Grant. The support of SLA is very gratefully acknowledged by the authors.

The book is divided into six parts:

1. Introduction, which outlines the purposes of the study and the methods used

2. A survey of the applications of the target technologies in library and information service environments

3. Applications from other fields that are closely related to library applications or directly relevant to information processing operations

4. A survey of applications in other fields that may have applicability, in some form, to libraries and other information services

5. General technologies implying artificial intelligence

6. Conclusions and implications

Introduction

Although artificial intelligence (AI) is a relatively new field, it has already accumulated an enormous literature, with several journals devoted exclusively to the subject. Furthermore, AI-related technologies have been applied, at least experimentally, to virtually all disciplines and fields of endeavor. Even within the library and information service arena, a substantial literature exists and a wide variety of applications have been described.

Because of the size, diversity, and scatter of the literature, it is extremely difficult for a manager to determine which, if any, of the applications may be transferable to the operations of a library, or other information service, now or in the foreseeable future. This problem is compounded by the fact that much of the literature is theoretical or speculative, and it is often difficult to determine whether a "system" really exists in an operational sense or exists only on paper. Furthermore, the literature on AI is one of extremes. On the one hand, we have authors who maintain that computers can be made to do virtually anything that humans can. At the other end of the scale are those who believe, equally strongly, that the claims for AI have been grossly exaggerated and that machines can *never* do anything that is truly intelligent.

The objective of the study reported here was to gain enough familiarity with developments in AI and related technologies to be able to advise the information service community on what can be applied today and what one might reasonably expect to be applicable to library and information services in the near future.

The emphasis, then, is on systems that are actually operational now—systems that have been incorporated into an everyday working situation rather than those that are at experimental or prototype stages. Also, in assessing the relevance of technologies, we have paid particular attention to applicability in a digital library environment since it seems inevitable that libraries of all types will be dealing more and more with network-accessible electronic sources and less and less with sources of information in printed form. Finally, we deal in greater detail with potentially relevant applications outside the library field—both because the systems are more likely to be fully operational and because they are less likely to be known to the library community.

Although the bibliography contains many references, it was never our intention to make it complete in any sense. Since our emphasis throughout has been on systems that are actually operating, and since almost none of the effort put into expert system development within the library community has resulted in fully operating systems, we have reviewed only a representative selection of the studies within the library/information center field.

In preparing the report, the authors surveyed the complete spectrum of applications of the technologies under consideration, with one notable exception: education. The field of computer-based education is so enormous in itself that it would have required a completely disproportionate amount of time to review. Moreover, apart from the education/training of staff and users, this field has no obvious applications to the operations of libraries and other information services.

Scope of the study

At the moment, computers can do certain things much better than humans can: operate with complete consistency, "remember" an infinite quantity of data, search or otherwise process enormous quantities of text, perform incredibly complex calculations, and so on. Humans can do other things much better than computers can. For example, we can reason; make decisions based on experience, inference, and "feelings" (and not solely on the basis of accumulated data); and we can learn from our experiences. While there is no universally accepted definition of "artificial intelligence," those who work in the field seek to develop computer systems capable of doing some of the things that humans now do better.[1] Fenly (1992), himself a librarian, offers one of the clearest statements relating to the scope of AI: "...computer programs have been developed which exhibit human-like reasoning, which may be able to learn from their mistakes, and which quickly and cleverly perform tasks normally done by scarce and expensive human experts" (Page 52).

Several areas of research and application are now considered to fall within the field of artificial intelligence. Figure 1, from Alberico and Micco (1990), gives a good idea of this coverage.

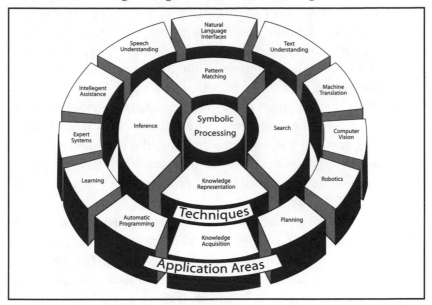

Figure 1 One possible classification of the AI field
From Alberico and Micco (1990) by permission of Penton Media, Inc.

It is obvious that many of the application areas identified in the diagram could have impact on libraries, particularly if operating largely in an electronic environment. Some other elements in the diagram are worth special attention. First, the field of "natural language processing" (NLP) is now frequently subsumed under "artificial intelligence," although it is doubtful if most processing of text (e.g., based on simple word occurrences) can be considered to involve any level of machine intelligence. The applications of NLP represented in the diagram either demand some level of intelligence (text understanding) or imply it (natural language interfaces may or may not be intelligent). This report does not deal with all aspects of NLP but focuses on the less routine applications, especially if they can be interpreted as incorporating intelligence and, obviously, have possible relevance to library operations and services.

The other term in Figure 1 that needs to be singled out is "expert systems." A review of the literature of artificial intelligence will reveal that much of it deals, in one way or another, with expert systems. Moreover, virtually all of the AI literature of direct relevance to libraries falls in the expert system category and *all* implementations of AI within the library field itself are of the expert system type.

The fact is that expert systems, while they seem to fit nicely into the Figure 1 categorization, really have a dimension different from that of the other elements of the diagram. Expert systems can be applied to most of the other areas represented: to planning, machine translation, text and speech understanding, the provision of intelligent assistance, the application of natural language interfaces, and so on. Because of their pervasive nature, expert systems receive special emphasis in this book.

As many readers will already know, an expert system has three principal components: a knowledge base, an inference engine, and a user interface. The inference engine is an intermediary between the knowledge base and the user interface. In essence, it operates on the knowledge in the knowledge base, frequently through a series of pre-established rules, in order to interact with the user, presenting questions, reminders, recommendations, and suggested answers or solutions.

Many software "tools" are now available commercially for the implementation of the inference engine and certain aspects of the user interface, and to provide a logical structure for the knowledge base. They are referred to under a variety of names: shells, knowledge-based system generators, software engineering tool suites, or simply implementation "environments." At least one major software tool, developed by a U.S. government agency, is in the public domain, although several commercial enhancements have been made to it.

Some of the software tools available are designed for a particular type of application (e.g., accounting, scheduling) while others are intended to be general-purpose (i.e., adaptable to most applications and knowledge bases). Some general-purpose expert system software can be bought very cheaply.

The knowledge base itself is application-specific; that is, it must be constructed and maintained by the institution implementing the expert system. To take a hypothetical example, suppose that an information center wanted to implement a system capable of answering certain questions on the thermophysical properties of materials. It might be able to identify software appropriate to use in the inference engine, to structure the knowledge base, and to implement the user interface. The center, however, would need to build the knowledge base (or import it from elsewhere), to organize it according to the requirements of the development software, and to keep it current. Updating of the knowledge base could also require changes to be made to the user interface.

While much development software is available for purchase, there are few systems in any field that are truly "off the shelf"—i.e., systems that can be bought for immediate implementation with little or no further development work needed—although more and more are appearing in specialized applications.

In theory at least, the manager wishing to apply an expert system to some information center operation or service has the following options available:

1. Buy an off-the-shelf system (very unlikely for most applications in the near future)

2. Buy the development software and build the system in-house

3. Contract with a knowledge engineering company (of which there are an increasing number) to develop the system

Regrettably, the terminology in this field is rather confusing. An expert system, as its name implies, is intended to capture some body of expertise and to make it available in a form useful to those who are less than expert in this area. Carried to its logical conclusion, the system becomes a substitute for the expert.[2] For obvious reasons, such systems are sometimes referred to as *knowledge-based* systems. However, a system can be knowledge-based without satisfying the other requirements for being an expert system as defined earlier. For example, the Hepatitis Knowledge Base, developed over several years by the National Library of Medicine, but no longer kept up-to-date, could be considered a knowledge-based system but not an expert system, even though the knowledge base was constructed by true experts. This is because it lacked the inference engine that is now considered an essential component of what we now think of as an "expert system." Clearly, it *would* satisfy the definition if it were fitted with software capable of aiding a physician in the diagnosis and differentiation of various forms of hepatitis.

Because many expert systems operate on the basis of rules (especially those of the "if ... then" type), they are sometimes referred to as *rule-based* systems. However, not all have a rule-based structure.

Almost all expert systems are designed to be interactive. They are not "black boxes" that spew out answers or solutions on the basis of a single input. Generally they require the user to refine the input (by something as simple as a menu selection or perhaps a more sophisticated conversational interaction), perhaps several times, before a possible solution is reached.

For the purpose of this book, expert system technology will be accepted as a branch of artificial intelligence, even though very few expert systems exhibit true intelligence (e.g., learn from their own mistakes).[3] The ability of a computer system to learn from experience is sometimes referred to as "machine learning." Langley and Simon (1995) review achievements in this field, including several diverse applications.

Methods

The study was conducted by means of five principal tasks:

1. Database searches

2. Document acquisition

3. Mail, e-mail, and telephone contacts

4. Consultation of various, relevant Web sites

5. Visits to organizations whose work appeared to be of special interest

The first searches were performed in the databases most closely related to library and information science, namely Library Literature, ERIC, Library and Information Science Abstracts (LISA), and Information Science Abstracts. Because these databases are close to our interests, very broad searches were conducted under *artificial intelligence* or *expert system(s)* or *neural networks.*[4]

These searches retrieved many thousands of citations. The results were reviewed online and only the more promising items were printed out. Even after this online screening, several hundred cita-tions/abstracts were printed for further examination.

A second set of searches was performed in the Wilson Business Periodical Index, Wilson Applied Science and Technology, and the Current Contents databases. Based on the results of the earlier searches, a much more refined strategy was possible. In particular, this second set of searches focused on terms likely to retrieve items of most potential relevance to the information service community; *text generation, intelligent text, intelligent agents, text interpretation, text understanding,* and *intelligent interfaces* are examples. After online screening, an additional 131 citations were printed out.

A third group of searches was performed in the following data-bases: INSPEC, Compendex, NTIS, Computer Select, and ABI/Inform, again using the refined strategy.

A final group of searches was performed in the databases outside the library/information science area. These searches employed broad terms for *artificial intelligence, expert systems,* and *natural language processing,* combined with *library* terms, including specific applications such as *reference, cataloging, information retrieval, collection develop-ment, acquisitions,* and *subject indexing.*

Through these searches (all limited to the latest 10-year period), many thousands of bibliographic records were reviewed to get the broadest possible overview of the scope of AI/ES technologies, espe-cially those in practical application, and to identify uses that might have relevance to library-related activities.

Items of greatest potential interest were obtained as photocopies or by borrowing the materials from the libraries of the University of Illinois, University of Michigan, and elsewhere. A few journals and conference proceedings dedicated to AI/ES applications were also reviewed cover to cover.

Altogether, many hundreds of items were examined. Some idea of the scope of the review can be obtained by scanning the bibliography, although only a small number of the items reviewed were actually cited.

Based on articles reviewed, a letter requesting further information was sent to companies claiming products or services in the AI or expert system arena if they seemed to be of particular interest (Appendix 1). A letter was also sent to authors who had described systems of potential interest to us, along with a brief questionnaire (Appendices 2 and 3). In particular, the latter was intended to determine the present status of the system described. The response rate was disappointing, necessitating further approaches by personal letter, telephone, and e-mail.

The authors originally proposed to visit institutions whose work appeared to have special interest. However, as the project progressed, it became obvious that this would not be a good use of project funds—systems of particular interest could usually be accessed remotely or demonstration disks were available to us. Moreover, centers of interest were widely dispersed geographically. Consequently, few actual visits were necessary. A single site visit was made, to Columbus, Ohio, because this allowed demonstrations and discussions at three institutions: Ohio State University, Chemical Abstracts Service, and OCLC.

Endnotes

1.   For a detailed discussion of the boundaries of artificial intelligence, see Simon (1995).

2.   In the final section of the book we discuss why this substitution may be infeasible and undesirable.

3. Many research projects seek to develop expert systems that are more intelligent. For example, "apprentice-based" approaches, or "learning apprentice" programs, are intended to allow the system to refine its own knowledge base by observing and analyzing the problem-solving steps of users (Mahadevan et al., 1993). Elofson (1995) gives an example of the apprentice-based approach.

4. Neural networks or, more correctly, artificial neural networks (ANN), are based on a highly interconnected network of nodes that process data numerically rather than symbolically. The processing of data, through interactions among the nodes, resembles the excitation and interaction of neurons within the brain. ANNs, which have the ability to learn from experience, may be incorporated into expert systems or other systems claiming artificial intelligence. They are not treated as a separate category in this report. Good explanations of neural networks appear in Rumelhart et al. (1994) and Chapter 17 of Quantrille and Liu (1991). Typical applications are discussed in Widrow et al. (1994), and Woelfel (1993) gives a very readable account of their potential value in policy research in general.

CHAPTER 1

Applications Within Libraries and Other Information Service Operations

Within the library/information service field, expert systems have been applied, at least experimentally, in several areas, namely:

1. Cataloging

2. Subject indexing

3. Acquisitions and collection development

4. Reference services

    a. Referral of users to appropriate information sources

    b. Selection of a database to search for a particular information need

    c. Development of a search strategy for database searching

The application of expert systems to other services or operations has been discussed but not implemented. Overviews of expert systems in library applications, with extensive bibliographies, are provided by Hanne (1997) and Zainab and DeSilva (1998).

Cataloging

All aspects of cataloging, other than subject cataloging, tend to be based on well-established rules. Cataloging, then, should be a library activity that is well suited to an expert system approach, and many articles, chapters or reports have been written on the subject. Almost all are purely theoretical or speculative, discussing the problems or potentials without actually implementing anything. While a few actual experiments have been conducted, they have mostly been paper exercises, modeling the expert system to determine the problems involved, rather than true implementations.

Given the title page of a book (front and back) in electronic form, it seems theoretically possible for a computer to determine author, title, publisher, edition, date, and, possibly, other elements used in descriptive cataloging. In practice, this is not at all an easy problem to solve.

Jeng (1987, 1991) studied some facets of the problem intensively. She analyzed the data appearing on about 200 title pages to determine what visual and linguistic cues human experts use in descriptive cataloging. Weibel and colleagues, at OCLC, carried this a little further by developing a small rule-based system and using a sample of title pages in electronic form (Weibel et al., 1989; Vizine-Goetz et al., 1990). The rules allowed some descriptive elements, such as publisher and place of publication, to be identified automatically at a high level of accuracy (around 80 percent), but they were much less successful with other elements. The work performed at OCLC and the work of Jeng both reveal that many decisions and distinctions that are very easy for the human cataloger to make may be far from easy to delegate successfully to a machine—one example is the distinction between title and subtitle.

Sandberg-Fox (1972, 1990) studied the problems involved in the automatic determination of "main entry" for a book but did not implement an actual system. Svenonius and Molto (1990) developed algorithms for the same purpose, and tested them, but again did not actually implement a system. The success of their algorithms varied with type of book (much less successful for scholarly books than for non-scholarly) and type of main entry (quite successful for personal main entry, moderately successful for title main entry, less so for corporate body main entry). Since they worked with relatively few title pages and used name authority files in the recognition process, it is not surprising that they got better than 80 percent recognition for 704 personal names and 374 corporate names.

Molto and Svenonius (1991) agreed with Weibel (1992) that OCR scanning of title pages to convert to ASCII format was not necessarily a trivial task.

The National Library of Medicine experimented with a small prototype expert system for determining the correct form of an author's name (Weiss, 1994). After 2½ years, and an investment of around $130,000, the project was discontinued. It was determined that the cost of transforming this to a real operating tool would be considerable. Moreover, the cataloging rules themselves were judged to be not well suited for machine interpretation, a conclusion reached by most of the other investigators in this area. See Meador and Wittig (1991) and Davies (1992) for other discussions of cataloging rules and their suitability for expert systems applications.

Ercegovac and Borko (1992a) implemented a prototype of an expert system to aid the cataloging of maps. The system developed, Mapper, was evaluated in a laboratory setting (Ercegovac and Borko, 1992b). It was determined, not surprisingly, that library school students, with no previous experience in the cataloging of maps, could do better with the system than without it.

Expert systems for selection of main and added entries were constructed at the University of Linköping (Hjerppe and Olander, 1989), but this did not lead to the implementation of an operating system. The experience of the investigators on this project brought them to the following significant conclusion: "An operational expert system for cataloging is technically feasible but would not be cost-effective for most libraries at present. In order to perform as well as an expert human cataloger an expert system would require computer resources far beyond the means of libraries in general" (Page 38). They do point out, however, that further technological developments could change this situation.

Smith et al. (1993) have produced algorithms for selection of main and added entries; the expert system in which they are incorporated is designed primarily for teaching cataloging in library schools.

The QUALCAT project (Ayres et al., 1994) had a more limited objective: the detection of duplicate catalog records and the selection of the duplicate that appears to be of higher quality. The investigators conclude that an expert system approach is feasible but there are limits to what can be achieved, due partly to characteristics of the MARC records.

None of the experiments on the automation of descriptive cataloging has produced a significant prototype system, much less a truly operational one, and virtually all who have studied the area agree that not a whole lot has been achieved. Jeng and Weiss (1994), for example, point out that "no system has been able to achieve satisfactory performance in practice," and Weibel (1992) sees a "thread of unreality" in much of the research. Fenly (1992), who assessed the promise of expert system technologies for application at the Library of Congress, concluded that "genuine expert systems, with the depth and power to solve substantial and meaningful problems, are time-consuming and costly to develop."

Despite the rather poor results achieved so far in descriptive cataloging, some investigators are still highly optimistic. For example, Schmidt and Putz (1993) claimed to be developing a system, CAROL (Cataloging by Automated Recognition of Literature), that "will significantly accelerate the cataloging process in libraries by automatically creating the catalog entry from a scanned title page." As of March 1993, they had worked only with title pages of doctoral theses and had not performed a thorough evaluation.

More recently, Sauperl and Saye (1999) reviewed the progress in expert systems for cataloging, and came to two major conclusions:

1. Although rules for descriptive cataloging are quite comprehensive and detailed, they are still insufficient to permit a comprehensive expert system knowledge base to be developed.

2. The graphic and visual characteristics of title pages and their idiosyncrasies continue to pose problems for the automatic recognition of descriptive access points.

They conclude that new tools are not likely to replace human catalogers, whose expertise ranges well beyond formal cataloging rules, requiring interpretation and judgement based on their education, general knowledge, and experience.

Subject indexing

This section of the report, more than most others, presents significant problems relating to scope. Work on "automatic indexing" goes back almost 40 years. Using a computer for "extraction indexing" (also known as "derivative indexing") has been quite successful, and some fully operating systems do exist. In this type of indexing, computer programs are written to extract words, phrases, or sentences from text such that these extracts are good indicators of the content of the complete text. Programs of this type usually work on the basis of statistical (word or phrase frequency), positional, or linguistic (e.g., part of speech) criteria.

Commercially available software will perform automatic extraction indexing based on statistical criteria or a combination of statistical and syntactic criteria. For example, CBR Generator (a product of Inference Corp.) will extract keywords from text and weight them on the basis of various statistical criteria (frequency in the item, frequency in the database as a whole, number of possible meanings of the word).

"Assignment indexing" by computer—i.e., assigning to a document subject headings, descriptors, or other terms from a controlled vocabulary—is much more difficult. Programs for automatic assignment indexing usually operate on the basis of a "word profile" for each descriptor; the descriptor is assigned if the text of a document (or, more likely the title or abstract) matches its word profile above some level. While operational systems of this kind have also been developed, they usually perform on relatively small controlled vocabularies. There is no system for completely automatic assignment indexing that operates with a controlled vocabulary of several thousand terms, which is typical of databases of the ERIC, MEDLINE, COMPENDEX, or INSPEC type, although large-scale machine-aided indexing systems do exist (see *Expert system approaches* on the next page).

With very few exceptions, the systems developed have been intended for machine-aided indexing rather than human replacement. That is, they suggest terms to the indexer, but the human may need to add to or delete from the computer's selection.

The literature on automatic or semi-automatic (machine-aided) indexing is vast and, it would be pointless to try to review it here (see Lancaster, 1998, for a review that is more complete). Almost all is outside the scope of this report: the algorithms that extract or assign terms exhibit little that can be considered truly intelligent. While machine-aided indexing systems might qualify as expert systems in that they try to help the less-experienced indexer to perform at the level of an expert, most do not meet the other expert system criteria outlined earlier—e.g., they lack a true inference engine—and they may not involve true interaction with the indexer.

This section, then, will be restricted to a discussion of true expert system approaches or approaches that can be considered, in some sense, intelligent. As true with other sections of the book, emphasis is on systems that are operational or, at least, semi-operational, since hundreds of experimental approaches occur in the literature.

A later section of the book, headed Intelligent Text Processing, should also be examined by those interested in computer-aided indexing since it deals with text categorization, text extraction, and other operations that can be considered indexing or indexing-related techniques.

Expert system approaches

The more specialized the indexing task, the more likely it is that it will be a cost-effective candidate for a true expert system approach. That is, real experts may be needed to understand and categorize certain texts or artifacts in order to index them effectively. Since the time of these experts will be costly, a system that aids lower-level personnel in performing at least some of the indexing could be a good investment. For example, Swaby (1991) gives a rather complete description of a system designed for the identification of microfossils. While not a conventional indexing situation, the principle is similar in that the operator, not an expert, is involved in the categorization of objects. The system is interesting in its use of a combination of text and graphics to aid the identification task. The user identifies the fossil at hand by viewing images of fossils on the screen along with their associated attributes and attribute values. The system operates in a way similar to that of a (medical) diagnostic system: based on the attributes selected as applying to the fossil at hand, the system leads the non-expert user to the most likely identification.

Tway and Riedel (1996) describe a somewhat similar system, COREX-PERT, designed to allow non-experts to describe (essentially "index") sediment cores drawn from ocean floors. The technician users complete data-entry screens to describe various characteristics of the sample at hand, using all the characteristics of the knowledge base (including photographs of sediment components and other visual aids) to assist this task. The system is referred to as an "intelligent data entry" system and some level of intelligence is built in to avoid errors. For example, the system checks for anomalies in the data entered—such as an anomalously high or low concentration of a particular mineral or the appearance together of two minerals that normally do not co-occur. Moreover, the technician need not directly identify all the mineral types or fossil groups occurring in the sample, but only the most important. The program can deduce the probability of occurrence of other elements (on the basis of the major elements known to be present or on recorded conditions such as water depth or geographic location). COREXPERT was developed for Scripps Institution of Oceanography but its use has been discontinued, partly due to lack of funds but also because it was "a victim of its own success": the technicians using the system became sufficiently knowledgeable that they could operate without it (Riedel, 1996). This is a fairly common fate for expert systems in such specialized applications.

Research on online machine-aided indexing applied to books, articles, and other publications goes back more than 30 years (see, for example, Bennett, 1969, and Bennett et al., 1972). Online aid can take several forms: suggesting terms to indexers (e.g., based on title, abstract, or other text manipulated by the computer or on the basis of terms already entered by the indexer), flagging certain indexer errors (e.g., terms not in the system vocabulary or invalid term combinations), substituting acceptable terms for unacceptable ones, and interfacing with the database to allow an indexer to find how certain terms have been used in the past or how certain items have been indexed in the past.

Online indexing systems in current operational environments offer varying degrees of help and sophistication. For example, the present system in use at the National Library of Medicine, AIMS (Automated Indexing and Management System), includes the following capabilities: for any headings input by an indexer it will, on command, show which subheadings may be used with it; display term annotations and scope notes; use cross-references to convert from a nonpreferred term or abbreviation to a preferred one; display portions of the controlled vocabulary hierarchically or alphabetically; and display a small set of generally applicable terms ("check tags") from which an indexer can select. To a very limited extent, it will prompt the indexer to assign a term based on one already assigned.

More sophisticated machine-aided indexing systems go beyond these capabilities to, for example, partially index an item or, at least, suggest terms to an indexer. An early system of this type is described by Martinez et al. (1987). Another example, called CAIN, was developed for use with AGREP, the European Community's database of ongoing agricultural research projects. Project descriptions include titles, abstracts, and uncontrolled terms indicative of the project scope. CAIN will match this text against two controlled vocabularies (AGROVOC and the CAB Thesaurus) and suggest candidate terms from these sources (Friis, 1992). Some other operating systems have similar capabilities. In the case of systems operating with short texts (e.g., cables) and/or relatively small controlled vocabularies, systems of this kind may be capable of doing much of the indexing correctly before the human indexer reviews to make any necessary corrections or additions.

A fully operational machine-aided indexing system on a large scale exists at NASA's Center for Aerospace Information (CAI), as described by Silvester et al. (1993). A knowledge base of phrases likely to occur in the aerospace literature (115,000 entries as of 1993) is used to map to NASA thesaurus terms. That is, the occurrence of these phrases in input text (usually titles and abstracts) leads the system to produce a list of candidate descriptors for indexer review. Related work at CAI has developed procedures for mapping to terms in the NASA thesaurus from terms assigned to records by other agencies and using other vocabularies (Silvester et al., 1993).

There remains considerable interest in automatic indexing for small specialized applications, especially in the biomedical field. In one example (Borst et al., 1992), the text of patient-discharge summaries is analyzed in order to assign relevant clinical descriptors automatically. Somewhat similar is a system, described by Oliver and Altman (1994), that will analyze medical records and assign SNOMED (Systematized Nomenclature of Human and Veterinary Medicine) terms to them.

Lirov and Lirov (1990) describe an expert system designed to assist in the production of specialized subject bibliographies. Once bibliographic records are retrieved and downloaded from an online database, the system will aid in the production of author and subject indexes; the keywords by which the bibliography is to be arranged are matched against descriptors in the bibliographic record.

Completely automatic assignment indexing (i.e., with no human intervention) for article-length texts dealing with complex subject matter (e.g., in medicine, chemistry, or physics) is far from realization, especially when the controlled vocabulary used is a very large one, so work continues to produce more sophisticated expert systems to aid the indexer. A notable example was MedIndEx, which was under development at the National Library of Medicine for a number of years (Humphrey, 1992). This was a conventional frame-based expert system approach. The user, who need not be an experienced indexer but should have at least some understanding of the medical literature and its terminology, is led to various relevant frames (e.g., type of disease, type of treatment) and prompted to complete them effectively. The system can prompt an indexer to assign a particular term and can also correct the indexer when a term is used inappropriately. For example, an indexer who assigns a neoplasm (cancer) term reflecting the site of the disease (e.g., *bone neoplasms*) can be reminded to assign a companion term representing the histologic type of the neoplasm (e.g., *adenocarcinoma*). Or, the indexer who assigns an inappropriate combination, such as *femur* and *bone neoplasms*, can be informed of the correct term, in this case *femoral neoplasms*. MedIndEx has never been implemented in an operational setting.

More recently, experiments at the National Library of Medicine have incorporated components of the Unified Medical Language System (UMLS) and its associated resources into an automatic indexing procedure (Wright et al., 1999). They describe how a natural language processing tool, called MetaMap, is used to automatically map words or phrases from full-text, SGML-encoded medical documents to concepts in the UMLS Metathesaurus. The Metathesaurus concepts identified by MetaMap are then input to another program called MetaMap Indexing (MMI) which provides a ranking of concepts based on their frequency and position of occurrence in the documents. Furthermore, SGML markup is exploited to hierarchically index documents at several levels of structure, thus facilitating retrieval on the most relevant sections in a given document. Indexing accuracy was evaluated by an

expert human indexer, and deemed adequate; a more formal evaluation has not yet been published.

Other systems have been developed to assist in the training of
indexers rather than to aid the indexing process on a day-to-day
basis; one system of this type, CAIT (Computer-Assisted Indexing
Tutor), was developed for the National Agricultural Library.

"Intelligent" indexing

Any computer-based system that helps in the task of subject indexing can be thought of as an expert system, at least in the loosest sense
of that term, especially if it helps a less-experienced person to approx-
imate the work of an expert indexer. And systems that suggest terms
to indexers, or correct certain indexer errors, can be considered to
offer at least a modicum of "intelligence."

It is doubtful that one can consider programs that merely extract terms
from text, or even those that do fairly routine matches between text strings
and controlled terms, as intelligent, although some of the programs discussed in a later section, Intelligent Text Processing, are perhaps more so,
especially those that will look for the occurrences of certain topics in text,
extract the information, and enter it into some form of template.

Some systems or programs described in the literature, however,
are referred to as "artificially intelligent." Examples can be found in
Driscoll et al. (1991) and Jones and Bell (1992).

The system described by the latter two authors is designed to
extract words or phrases from text in order to form index entries. It
works largely on the basis of stored lists: of words to be ignored, of
words/phrases/names of known interest, and lists to aid in the dis-
ambiguation of homographs, to conflate singular/plural forms, and
to allow simple parsing (a list of word endings). The lists are combined to form a dictionary, which also includes information to allow
other facilities such as limited generic posting.

The system described by Driscoll et al. is also designed to find useful
index terms in text. Text is processed against a list of more than 3,000
phrases. Occurrence of one of these in a text triggers the use of insertion
and deletion rules. The deletion rules merely avoid further processing of
words or phrases that are ambiguous, whereas the insertion rules can

generate a limited set of sought terms (to complete a "template") by implication. For example, the words "time," "over," and "target" will generate AIR WARFARE if they appear within x words of each other.

Systems of the type described by Driscoll et al. and by Jones and Bell are ingenious. They may be capable of performing extraction indexing or extraction with limited assignment, at a level comparable to that achieved by human indexers and at less cost. At the very least, they are useful for producing candidate terms for human review. Nevertheless, one cannot really agree that they exhibit true intelligence. The same may be said for programs that develop "thesauri" and other searching aids on the basis of term co-occurrence (e.g., Chen et al., 1995).

Neural networks have also been applied to automatic indexing of documents by Chen et al. (1998c) and by Chung et al. (1998). In both cases, terms extracted from a document are used as "input patterns" to the network. A parallel spreading activation process eventually converges on another set of terms that are strongly related to the input terms. Although these approaches are referred to as "semantic indexing," they make use of statistical, not truly semantic, approaches. At present they both exist in experimental form, and evaluation results, in the form of recall and precision values, show some promise. However, Chung et al. (1998) state that "from a practical perspective, the current technology may require human interaction to assure the quality of the resulting indexes."

A specialized application of increasing interest is that of the indexing of photographs and other images. Rowe and colleagues at the U.S. Naval Postgraduate School form one research group that has concentrated on this area for several years. Their approach uses a combination of text (picture captions) and pixel-level image processing. A neural net method is used for region classification applied to photographs, and automatic parsing procedures are applied to the captions. Their work includes the indexing of photographs forming part of Web pages (Rowe and Guglielmo, 1993; Rowe, 1994, 1999; Rowe and Frew, 1996, 1997). Yu and Wolf (1997) describe another system that performs tagging of images off-line using a neural network algorithm and answers queries online using only the tags. In contrast, St. Clair et al. (1998) report on a more sophisticated system than the automatic tagging approach just described. Their system learns features of a graphic object and can compare all match objects regardless of their orientation or scale.

Approaches to the indexing of collections of paintings, and other art objects, are being pursued by various research groups. For example, Ozaki et al. (1996) describe an approach that incorporates information on what is depicted and how it is depicted (e.g., spatial orientation) as well as on aesthetic factors, such as color and style. More sophisticated approaches to the indexing and retrieval of art objects (e.g., searching for a painting that resembles a sketch input by a searcher) are mentioned later in the book (see Computer vision on page 101).

Jones and Roydhouse (1995) describe an intriguing case-based system for indexing and retrieving of meteorological data. Faced with a current weather situation, a meteorologist can search for past situations of similar conditions. A map of the present conditions (see Figure 2) can be used as a query; the system will then rank earlier situations in order of similarity (see Figure 3). Each graphical object in the query (Figure 2), such as location of the pressure center and its magnitude, is converted into a symbolic representation that is used to search the database where earlier cases are also represented symbolically.

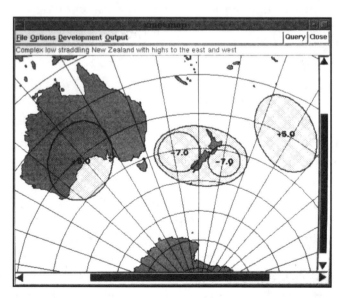

Figure 2 A query made to a meteorological database. The query requests a complex low-pressure system over New Zealand with high-pressure systems to east and west.

From Jones and Roydhouse, "Intelligent Retrieval of Archived Meteorological Data," *IEEE Expert,* 10(6), 1995, 50-57. © 1995, IEEE.

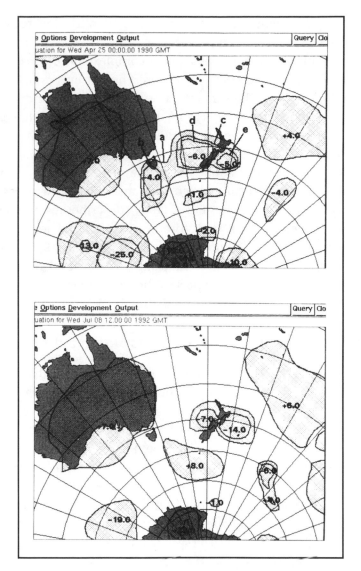

Figure 3   Two weather maps retrieved in response to the Figure 2 query
From Jones and Roydhouse, "Intelligent Retrieval of Archived Meteorological Data," *IEEE Expert*, 10(6), 1995, 50-57. © 1995, IEEE.

A more complex image indexing and retrieval problem is that associated with remote-sensing data from orbiting satellites. Cromp and Dorfman (1992) discuss the problem and describe a spatial data management system "capable of storing and retrieving records of image data regardless of their source."

An indexing situation of even greater complexity is that associated with sound databases. Foote (1999) presents an overview of audio information retrieval; he surveys current technologies and suggests future directions, such as increasing the breadth of audio that can be processed as well as integrating audio and video retrieval. Modern methods for synthesizing and archiving sounds electronically can make large numbers of sounds available to the musician, but the retrieval of a particular sound from such an archive presents a significant problem. Feiten and Günzel (1994) describe an approach to indexing and retrieval of sounds through use of neural networks. The retrieval index is created automatically. Kataoka et al. (1998) describe a neural network approach to indexing and retrieval of music in which the user can input any part of the melody remembered; they claim 91.5 percent accuracy in identifying the music correctly.

Acquisitions and collection development activities

An obvious potential application of expert systems within libraries is for the selection of booksellers or other vendors of library materials. Carried to its logical conclusion, a system might be developed to select a vendor automatically based on past performance in the supply of publications of a particular type. Such a capability would be especially valuable in the acquisition of materials that are less routine—conference proceedings, certain technical reports, publications in certain languages, publications from certain countries, and so on.

Pontigo et al. (1992) have described a type of expert system designed to select vendors in this way. The system has a learning capability—the performance factors associated with each vendor are updated automatically as the system gathers further data on vendor performance. In fact, the system is designed to rank potential vendors by the probability that they will be able to supply a particular item needed.

A similar system, known as the Monographic Acquisitions Consultant, was developed at Iowa State University (Zager and Smadi, 1992; Hawks, 1994). The system was designed to optimize the decision on which vendors to go to for particular types of monographs. The knowledge base of the system includes both descriptive and evaluative data on each supplier. Descriptive data deal with type of publisher (foreign, university press, publisher of science materials) and relationship with the library (blanket order, approval plan, standing order, on exchange list), while the evaluative data cover aspects of service (delivery time, accuracy, discounts, shipping and handling charges, and so on). The evaluative elements can be weighted and the system can thus assign a composite numerical score to each vendor based on the company's previous performance for the library. As Hawks (1994) describes: "In the selection process, the vendor with the highest score who can supply a given type of material is recommended. Once a certain number of orders has been sent to that vendor in a given time period, the vendor with the next highest rating will be selected instead, supporting the library's goal of using multiple vendors" (Page 208).

This system and the one developed in Mexico by Pontigo et al. (1992) were implemented as prototypes but have not been used on a full production basis. Hardware problems and the cost involved in updating the knowledge base were mentioned as barriers to full adoption in Iowa, although it was shown that the system could save a considerable amount of professional time in the actual selection of vendors.

Along the same lines, but somewhat less ambitious, is a system developed at Pennsylvania State University to determine whether or not a particular title is likely to be received through one of the library's many approval plans (Brown, 1993). Criteria incorporated into the knowledge base, and used to determine probability of receipt, are publisher, subject, price, year of publication, and place of publication. Again, while a prototype was developed and tested, the system has not been fully implemented.

Other expert systems, designed to help library users satisfy their own needs, have also included document-ordering aids (e.g., Bianchi and Giorgi, 1986; Waldstein, 1986).

Systems have also been designed within the library community to aid in the selection process. Systems of this type have been discussed by Rada et al. (1987), Sowell (1989), Meador and Cline (1992), and Hall (1992).

Rada et al. have described an expert system approach to the selection of journals. While their objectives were somewhat different—the decision on whether or not a journal should be included in the MED-LARS database—the criteria built into their system (type of publisher, language, type of article, type of author, publication standards) would be among those relevant to a knowledge base designed to aid a librarian in journal-selection decisions. The system described was never really implemented and, indeed, seems to have existed only on paper (Backus, 1996). Hall (1992) discusses work undertaken to develop an expert system for selection of periodicals, but there is no evidence that it was actually implemented.

Meador and Cline describe a workstation designed to make readily accessible all of the information that a librarian might need in selection decisions: collection development guidelines, holdings and circulation data, financial data, and so on. While not an expert system per se, this approach can be considered as a first step toward the development of such a system.

Sowell describes a rudimentary expert system to aid in monograph selection, but he deals only in a very narrow subject area, and the prototype developed was tested with very few cases. The experimental system was discontinued.

DeBrower and Jones (1991) describe an application for which a simple expert system seems highly appropriate: making a decision as to which books donated to the library should actually be added to the collection. The system they developed at the Applied Physics Laboratory, Johns Hopkins University, and known as Gift Assistant, was designed to allow such decisions to be made by support staff rather than professional librarians. Since several hundred such donations are made to the library each year, it was considered that enough professional time could be saved to make the development worthwhile.

The aide using Gift Assistant is prompted to make the decision on the basis of classification number, age, number of copies already owned (if any), and whether or not copies owned are available on the shelf at the time the decision is made. Through use of the system, the library aide is able to make about 75 percent of the decisions without consulting a librarian. However, when evaluated against decisions that a professional librarian would make, the system can be considered only moderately successful. While the system could help the aide to successfully make about 83 percent of the decisions on what to reject, it was successful in only around 50 percent of the accept decisions.

A related technology to expert systems involves the creation of intelligent software agents (a more in-depth review of this subject appears later in the book). McKiernan (1998) describes the application of agent-based technology to the building of a collection development system. He describes the general functionalities of a profile agent, a search agent, an OPAC agent, a feedback agent, an ILL agent, and an acquisitions agent. This appears not to have gone beyond the discussion stage.

A system of more limited scope, which uses an expert system to locate potential suppliers of ILL-requested items at the Triangle Research Libraries in North Carolina, is described by Nye (1997), who speaks of two modules—one for borrowing and one for lending—but it is not clear whether there is any sort of real knowledge base within the system or whether it has really been implemented.

Reference services

Referral systems

The term "referral system," as used here, relates to systems that are designed to refer library users to information sources likely to provide the answer to a particular question of the factual or "information on" type. Within the library community, more work has been done on systems of this kind than on any other expert system application. Mostly such systems refer users to printed sources—i.e., conventional reference books—but other types of sources, such as those in CD-ROM form, can also be included in the knowledge base. The objective of such systems is obvious: to guide library users to a suitable source when a reference librarian is not available to help them. Some referral systems cover knowledge as a whole (as in the coverage of a general reference library) while others are restricted to highly specialized domains.

This type of system is conceptually similar to those designed to aid database selection (see later): both refer users to appropriate information sources—a database in one case, a printed tool (usually) in the other. Moreover, both types of systems operate in a very similar way: through use of menus. Menus lead the user from broad subject categories to successively narrower ones and may eventually restrict by other criteria such as type of information required (e.g., definition, statistical, biographical). Thus, a user might be led from Science (Menu 1) to Computer Science (Menu 2) to Artificial Intelligence (Menu 3) to Catalogs/Directories (Menu 4) and eventually be referred to Durkin's *Expert Systems: Catalog of Applications*. This hypothetical example is actually rather simplistic because most systems do not narrow to such an extent, with the result that the user is more likely to be referred to several possible sources rather than a single candidate.

Examples of referral tools developed in specialized subject areas include: ORFEO, dealing with opera but existing only as a prototype (Gerber, 1992); ANYTHING GOES, dealing with American musical theater and, again, only a prototype (Metzger, 1993); and Public Health Librarian (Chan and Carande, 1991), a reference advisory system in public health. Sears (1994) describes an application in the field of communications law but there is no evidence that the system was ever more than experimental. Vedder et al. (1989) discuss five "expert systems for business reference" but, in fact, only evaluated the suitability of various software (shells) for this application. Main and Weckert (1993) describe an Australian system applied to a community information service. It is designed to aid the selection of organizations capable of providing information or help needed by a library user, but it refers only to the type of organization suitable, not directly to the details of the organizations. As described, it is only a prototype.

Over the years, the National Agricultural Library has been responsible for developing several expert referral systems in highly specialized areas (Waters, 1992) including AquaRef (in aquatic sciences), later modified as Regis II (Bailey and Myers, 1991), and Plant Expert Advisor (Mason and Sample, 1992). They are somewhat different from the systems mentioned earlier. The Plant Expert Advisor incorporates a Windows-based interface and a multimedia CD-ROM designed to help a homeowner to select plants for landscaping. The system includes a substantial body of text and illustrations on the 960 plants covered, and users can search the database on various combinations of 26 characteristics: preferred soils, color of flowers, uses for the plant, and so on. REGIS II also incorporates a CD-ROM plus online connection and includes citations dealing with aquaculture and fisheries, text on African aquaculture, and lists of specialists in the subject area.

More conventional is the Government Documents Reference Aid, developed at Stanford University Libraries (Bailey and Myers, 1991; Harley and Knobloch, 1991). As its name implies, it helps library users to find appropriate state, federal, or foreign government documents. An earlier system dealing with government information sources, POINTER, developed at the State University of New York at Buffalo (K. F. Smith, 1990), was discontinued because of the effort needed to keep it up to date (Smith, 1996).

EELIAS (Electrical Engineering Literature and Information Advisory System), developed at Monash University, was designed as a reference tool but was somewhat different in purpose—it was to act as a kind of automated "pathfinder." In the field of electrical engineering, it helps library users to find recommended books, journals, standards, indexes, and other items, rather than focusing on their specific questions (Dabke and Thomas, 1992). A prototype was developed but discontinued because it was "very clumsy" to update (Thomas, 1996); hypertext and hypermedia approaches were determined to be preferable (Morrisey, 1992; Thomas and Hadgraft, 1996).[1]

Hardy (1993) describes a system, similar to those already mentioned, that deals with the area of legislative history. However, it was not designed for use in libraries but to assist an individual in finding sources and sections of sources needed to perform research in legislative history.

General referral systems—suitable for use in a general reference library—are Reference Expert, developed at the University of Houston (Bailey, 1992); Source Finder, developed at the University of Illinois; and COBRA (Computer Assisted Bibliographic Reference and Advisory System), developed at the University of Groningen (Bosman et al., 1994). These differ primarily in the number of sources included. COBRA claims to cover 7,000, Source Finder includes some 2,100, and Reference Expert only 340. Jörgensen and Jörgensen (1991) refer to a similar system designed for use by a small liberal arts college but it seems never to have been put into place. Another general reference system, Ask Alcuin, is described by Morgan (1997). It uses a question-and-answer format to direct users to appropriate print sources, online databases, and Web pages; a very preliminary version of this system can be found at http://www.lib.ncsu.edu/staff/morgan/alcuin.

A rather stringent evaluation of Reference Expert and Source Finder was performed (Su and Lancaster, 1995), using library school students as test subjects. Ten "real" reference questions, covering a wide range of subjects, were used in the study. The success of the students, using the expert systems, was judged on whether or not they were able to find reference sources for the test questions judged to be "as good" as sources selected by experienced reference librarians. Students were divided into two groups: those with previous experience in reference work and those with no previous experience. Whichever system was used, the more experienced students did no better with system aid than they did without it. Even with the less-experienced students, only one of the two systems improved on their unaided selection of reference sources. Compared with the expert reference librarian standard, one system allowed the complete group of library students to achieve 80 percent success, while the other allowed only 40 percent success. A major problem noted by Su and Lancaster (1995) is that the system menus are not sufficiently specific, leading to many candidate sources rather than focusing on one or two. They conclude that, at the present stage of development, systems of this kind could offer help to only the most inexperienced of library users.[2]

In very limited domains it should be possible to develop systems that actually answer user questions rather than simply point to potential sources of answers. Systems of this kind would be particularly suitable for knowledge bases that are static or that would change very slowly. For example, a system such as ORFEO would be more useful if it could directly answer questions about opera plots, settings, characters, composers, first performances, and so on. While work to develop question-answering systems in very limited fields has gone on for a long time (see, for example, Green et al., 1963), modern technologies make them much more feasible. For instance, Stock (1993) describes a hypermedia system, ALFRESCO, containing images of 14th century Italian frescoes and capable of answering a wide variety of questions concerning them, including the identification of characters or objects depicted in particular paintings.

Database selection

Several librarians have developed systems to help people decide which online database is most likely to satisfy a particular information need, and tools of this type have also been released commercially.

An early experimental system for database selection was developed by Thornburg (1987) as a doctoral research project. It is typical of many others that followed. Interactive menus were used to guide the user in selection of a database. Based on subject area indicated by the user, and the type of document required, her system would suggest a database and would calculate the probability that this database would be the best choice among the 18 available. While implemented, in the sense that it existed in hardware rather than paper, it did not go beyond a laboratory setting.

Trautman and von Flittner (1989) described a prototype that will give all databases included a composite numerical score earned on nine different attributes, including type of material covered, subject area, time span, language, and target audience. This seeming sophistication, however, is somewhat misleading. For almost all searches, the overriding factor in the selection of databases will be the match between the subject matter of the request and the subject coverage of the database (rather than type of document, language, or other attribute). In the prototype described, database coverage is represented only in general terms (derived, in fact, from categorizations in the published directories), not at the specific term level provided by the database indexes, so it will draw one's attention to the obvious databases rather than to those that are less obvious. As the authors point out, this tool may help the novice but is unlikely to be of much use to the expert searcher.

A.G. Smith (1991) describes an expert system with a more limited goal: selection of databases, accessible in New Zealand, to answer questions about New Zealand. Typical of other systems developed to aid database selection, this one, Kiwinet Advisor, works through use of menus that help the user to narrow the scope of the topic sought, in much the same way that the referral tools, described earlier, do. Kiwinet Advisor was later replaced with a system of wider scope, the New Zealand Reference Advisor. While still dealing with questions concerning New Zealand, it was expanded to include printed as well as electronic sources (Smith, 1992).

Zahir and Chang (1992) developed another system of this general type, known as Online-Expert, for the selection of business-related databases. It is more sophisticated than most in the procedures used to rank databases but, nevertheless, has not been developed beyond a prototype stage.

Researchers at the Loughborough University of Technology also produced tools for the selection of databases in the business area—specifically databases including information on companies within the U.K. (Morris, 1994; Morris et al., 1994; Tseng et al., 1994; Tseng et al, 1995). The prototype was not converted into a commercial system for lack of funding. Morris (1996) has pointed out that "With the way things have moved on, it is doubtful whether a commercial system would have been successful anyway." The researchers at Loughborough have now moved away from the expert systems area.

The 1980s did see the emergence of some commercially produced tools for database selection. The major product of this time was Easynet, developed by Telebase Systems, Inc. to provide access to several hundred databases accessible online through various vendors (Hu, 1987, 1988; McCarthy, 1986; O'Leary, 1988; van Brakel, 1988). Easynet was released in various versions, each intended for a particular audience, including one, Infomaster, offered by Western Union. Easynet offered several capabilities to the user of online information services, including access to a multitude of online sources through one log-on operation, a single billing procedure, and a common query language, as well as database selection. It too uses a menu approach to help a user narrow the scope of a search and to select an appropriate database.

Use of the Easynet/Infomaster menu, which incorporates type of materials covered by the databases, as well as subject area, can be illustrated by a simple example from Hu (1987), who wanted to find periodical articles on artificial intelligence. The first subject screen gave her a choice of six broad subject categories, from which she selected the category Computer,

Science, Technology. The next screen presented seven subdivisions of this broad area, from which Computer, Engineering, Technology was selected. This subdivision also had seven subdivisions, from which Computer was selected. The next screen offered three categories of computer information; (1) home, business, or educational use, (2) research and technical information; and (3) telecommunications. Hu selected the first of these, and the next screen offered a choice among the types of material covered: research and popular magazines, the full text of magazines, books on computers, encyclopedias, and a list of related databases. She chose the first of these and was then asked to enter the specific topic of the search. The terms ARTIFICIAL INTELLIGENCE *or* AI, when entered by Hu, led to the selection of the MICROCOMPUTER INDEX database, which was then searched, informing Hu that there were 461 items satisfying the search requirement.

The implication of this particular menu approach is that the terms input by the searcher, once the subject scope has been narrowed and type of material selected, will lead the user to the most appropriate database within that category. Hu's study, however, suggests that this is not true—that, for example, once a searcher has used the menu to narrow down to "databases of periodical articles on home, business or educational use of computers," the same database (in this case MICROCOMPUTER INDEX) may be selected, whatever terms are input by the searcher. In fact, Hu showed that a completely nonsensical string of characters, when entered in place of subject terms, led to the selection of the same database. It was not clear to her on what basis the final selection of databases was made; she suggests that commercial interests may play a part.

Easynet offered another feature: Easynet Scan. Once the searcher had narrowed the search as far as the menus will allow, he or she could enter search terms and get a display of the databases within the category, showing the number of times the term or combination of terms occurs in each, as well as the level of information offered by the database (bibliographic reference, abstract, or full text). Most displays thus generated would also include a "recommended database indicator (RDI)," which is a symbol indicating the database that the company developing the system recommends most strongly within a particular category, presumably because it is the obvious primary database for that category (ERIC for education, PAIS International for public and international affairs, and so on). In a series of four articles, Meyer and Ruiz (1990) studied the databases selected by Easynet users through the Scan feature. They concluded that the presence of an RDI in a display exerted more influence than any other factor, including cost, on user selection of a database. Users were influenced more by the RDI than even the number of times the search terms occurred in the database.

The analysis by Meyer and Ruiz casts further light on the results achieved by Hu. Almost without exception, the database selected in Hu's study was one bearing an RDI. It seems, then, that Easynet always selected the RDI database within a category or subcategory that was arrived at by the searcher whenever an RDI has been assigned to databases in that category/subcategory.

Hu (1987), in her rather thorough evaluation of Easynet, concluded that, with its aid, library school students could do as well as experienced librarians in the selection of databases. However, neither group did very well when compared with another standard: they tended to select the "obvious" databases and to overlook others (e.g., more specialized) that might be more appropriate. Roberts (1986) also reported that a search through Easynet could be more expensive than going directly to the vendor, at least for the cheaper databases, and Buxton (1988), discussing a European application of the system, reported longer search times and significantly increased costs.

Some individual vendors introduced their own interface approaches. For example, Dialog Information Services (now part of Knight-Ridder Information, Inc.) offered DIALOG Business Connection and DIALOG Medical Connection. Their primary purpose was not database selection but help to the user in developing a search strategy, which was then applied to all the databases in the group (all business or all medical).[3] These products were replaced by rather more sophisticated ones (e.g., Dialog's Business Base and Science Base) which use Windows-based menus to guide a user in database selection and search approach. Tools that help users to develop a strategy, with or without database-selection features, are dealt with in the next section of this book.

Those individuals who have studied or evaluated tools for database selection (and even those who have developed prototypes) generally agree that the experienced searcher can do better without them, especially if their use adds to overall search costs, but that they may be useful for the novice.

The database selectors referred to in this section were developed before the emergence of the Internet. The various tools developed to aid in searching Internet resources are dealt with later in the book.

Information retrieval

Intelligent interfaces to information systems are discussed in a later section of this report. Such interfaces access existing systems, with all their constraints and deficiencies, so they can only be as successful as the information retrieval system allows. Harman (1992) argues that attempts to develop more intelligent interfaces are inherently limited by the design of the underlying information retrieval (IR) system. For many years, IR research was done by a small community that had little impact on industry. The large commercial information services such as DIALOG were based on standard Boolean logic approaches to text matching and did not incorporate the results of IR research. Now IR techniques once found only in experimental systems have found their way into major information services, such as West Publishing's WIN system, the first natural language application in the commercial online environment (Pritchard-Schoch, 1993) and World Wide Web search engines (e.g., InfoSeek). It has long been recognized that Boolean logic poses problems for the typical user not specifically trained in searching, both in understanding the appropriate use of the logical operators and because all items matching the strategy are retrieved in a single, undifferentiated set. Now features once considered too esoteric for the typical user, such as natural language queries, ranked retrieval results, term weighting, query by example, and query formulation assistance, have become common in software for text retrieval and in Internet search engines.

The basic operation underlying most IR applications is to match a short piece of text, normally a query or user profile, against records in a database (where records may range from bibliographic citations to the full text of documents). Over four decades, a large number of diverse techniques for performing this basic operation have been proposed, developed, and implemented in an effort to provide more efficient and effective tools for locating items that the inquirer would consider relevant. Although it may not be appropriate to label more sophisticated IR systems "intelligent" in the sense that they exploit an understanding of the query and documents as a basis for selecting items likely to be relevant, such systems do make use of statistical and natural language processing techniques to enhance the matching process. Salton and McGill (1983), Frakes and Baeza-Yates (1992), Korfhage (1997) and Baeza-Yates and Ribeiro-Neto (1999) can be consulted for an explanation of many of the techniques that underly more sophisticated IR systems. Recent review articles highlighting developments in IR research and development include those by Kantor (1994) on information retrieval techniques, Spink and Losee (1996) on feedback in IR, and Efthimiadis (1996) on query expansion (the process of supplementing the original query with additional terms as a method for improving retrieval performance).

Croft (1995) summarizes the experience of the University of Massachusetts Center for Intelligent Information Retrieval (CIIR) in the area of industrial and government research priorities for IR system research and development. Priorities identified include relevance feedback (a process by which users identify relevant documents in an initial list of retrieved documents, and the system then creates a new query based on those sample relevant documents), multimedia retrieval (accessing image, video, and sound databases without text descriptions), more effective retrieval (enhanced recall—retrieving all relevant items—and precision—retrieving only the relevant items), vocabulary expansion (going beyond the terminology initially used in the query), efficient retrieval (developing algorithms that will operate in real-time, interactive systems), and distributed IR (merging multiple ranked lists to provide an integrated response to a query from multiple databases).

One example of software incorporating a variety of retrieval techniques is INQUERY, developed by CIIR (http://ciir.cs.umass.edu/inquerypage.html). The INQUERY query language and underlying Bayesian inference net model integrate natural language, Boolean, and proximity queries, including field-based retrieval. Output is ranked by the probability of satisfying the user's information need. INQUERY also has a sophisticated model for handling phrases. Long documents are retrieved based on both their entire content and their best passages. INQUERY has relevance feedback techniques for automatically modifying initial queries based on user-identified relevant documents. The INQUERY Web pages identify and provide links to a number of systems making use of the software, including the THOMAS project for U.S. legislation, the Library of Congress American Memory project for archival materials related to American culture and history, the U.S. Holocaust Memorial Museum library and archives, and the InfoSeek Web search service.

For the most part, the evaluation of IR systems has been carried out on relatively small collections of documents and queries. In 1992 the first of a series of evaluation exercises called TREC (Text REtrieval Conference) was launched in the U.S. (Harman, 1993 a, b), and these exercises have continued annually since then. What makes TREC notable in IR research is that the document collections used are large and the groups participating in this collaborative evaluation represent a "who's who" of IR research across the world, in both the academic and commercial sectors (Smeaton and Harman, 1997; Voorhees and Harman, 2000). The range of IR approaches tried within TREC is almost the complete range of IR techniques, including automatic thesauri, sophisticated term weighting, natural language techniques, relevance feedback, and advanced pattern matching (see the TREC Web site for more information on this series of evaluations, http://www-nlpir.nist.gov/TREC; the proceedings of these conferences are a rich source of information on retrieval techniques under development). What all these experiments have combined to show is that there is no single system or approach to IR that is the best or most effective, but certain techniques are proving useful. Such techniques are finding their way into the marketplace much faster now as they are incorporated in software for text retrieval and in Web search engines (Sparck Jones, 1995, 2000). Because they are commercial products, the implementation details are likely to be proprietary. Thus, one can observe in using an Internet search engine that the retrieved Web sites are ranked, but the specific algorithm used to accomplish this is not known. In addition these products regularly incorporate refinements and enhancements. Thus, comparative evaluation must be carried out on an ongoing basis to determine which engines yield the best results for particular categories of queries (Dong and Su, 1997).

System performance as measured in TREC (effectiveness measures of recall and precision) is only one (albeit important) part of the evaluation of a search engine. Other aspects are engineering issues (e.g., efficiency of operation for handling queries in real time) and usability. Powerful IR systems may be made more usable through the design of improved interfaces, as explained later in the section on intelligent interfaces.

Although one of the findings of the TREC experiments has been that natural language processing (NLP) techniques do not outperform statistical ones, a number of individuals continue to promote the use of NLP in IR (Feldman, 1999). Jones (1999) described the performance of DR-LINK, a commercial IR search tool based on linguistics, versus TARGET, based on relevance ranking. She concluded that, although DR-LINK did outperform TARGET, this could be explained by the simplistic nature of the queries and the limited number of test questions. A more thorough and definitive study of the state-of-the-art in natural language information retrieval is provided by Perez-Carballo and Strzalkowski (2000). They conclude, on the basis of their TREC-6 experiments, that "natural language processing can now be done on a fairly large scale and that its speed and robustness has improved to the point where it can be applied to real IR problems." However, it should be noted that the emphasis in natural language processing within information retrieval has been on "surface-oriented" processing, such as part of speech tagging, identification of noun phrases and their structure, and combination of NLP techniques with statistical ones. This contrasts with the deeper semantic processing of true natural language understanding (NLU) techniques from AI.

Other library applications

The applications dealt with so far in this section of the book are those to which most effort has been devoted within libraries and other information centers. Another area that has received minor attention is that of classification. Iyer and Giguere (1995) have done work toward development of an expert system to map from one classification scheme to another, in this case from the mathematics scheme of the American

Mathematical Society to the mathematics section of the Dewey Decimal Classification. They claim that "An interface that enables mathematicians to access library collections organized with the Dewey Decimal Classification using the AMS scheme as an interface will certainly be useful." Nevertheless, this type of application seems of very limited value.

Of more general interest would be an interactive system to aid in the actual assignment of class numbers. Some work of this type has been done but not on a very great scale. For example, Gowtham and Kamat (1995) developed a prototype system for classifying in the field of metallurgy using the Universal Decimal Classification. While much less ambitious and sophisticated than the MedIndEx system described earlier, the prototype they describe operates in a similar way in that it prompts the user to construct a class number having all the necessary facets (type of metal, property, type of process applied, and so on). Cosgrove and Weimann (1992) also discuss an expert system approach to classification by the UDC but from a theoretical perspective—there is no evidence that any system, even an experimental one, was implemented.

Significant work on automatic classification is now being performed at OCLC and is discussed and summarized by Vizine-Goetz (1998). The Scorpion project at OCLC is experimenting with the automatic classification of Web pages using the Dewey Decimal Classification (Thompson et al., 1997). Assignment is based on the matching of Web text against the text headings associated with the DDC class numbers using algorithms developed for use in Salton's SMART system.

Earlier, Larson (1992) had experimented on a small scale with the automatic assignment of class numbers from the Library of Congress Classification. His objective was different: the automatic assignment of a single number to a book based on titles and subject headings appearing in MARC records. As in the OCLC work, his algorithm ranks class numbers in order of probability of "correctness." Larson concluded that fully automatic classification may not be possible, although semi-automatic classification may be. That is, his program could produce a list of candidate (highly ranked) numbers from which a classifier could select the most appropriate one.

Research on automatic classification also takes place in fields beyond library science. For example, Bailin et al. (1993) have discussed work on the classification of software components (for a repository of reusable software); machine-learning capabilities are claimed. Savić (1995) deals with the possibilities for automatic classification of office correspondence.

Work on automatic thesaurus construction proceeds in a number of research centers, although these are outside the library field. The tools thus constructed, while they do reveal possibly useful relationships among terms, are much less highly structured than thesauri created by humans. Examples can be found in Gao et al. (1995), Chen et al. (1995), and Lu et al. (1995), and a commercial product making use of automatic thesaurus construction techniques, CLARIT (http://www.clarit.com), is widely available.

Conclusions

Many library-related applications of expert systems or "intelligent technologies" have been discussed in the literature, but this is extremely misleading. Systems that have progressed to an "operational" state—i.e., are functioning on a daily basis and providing a real service to library staff or users—are almost nonexistent. The literature is full of article titles suggesting that systems exist when, in fact, they never did or did only in a very limited sense.[4] In some cases the system existed only on paper. In the great majority of others, an experimental system was actually implemented but was never moved beyond the laboratory or prototype stage. In the worst of cases, an author reached by telephone could barely remember involvement in the project, or a person identified as the appropriate "contact" denied any knowledge of the work. The failure to develop real-life systems within the library sphere will be discussed in the Conclusions and Implications section of the book.

Endnotes

1. This is not the only example of a situation in which a formal expert system approach proved less satisfactory than an alternative. In a completely different environment (access to information in a collection of oncopathology slides), Vít et al. (1995) also abandoned an expert system shell in favor of a hypertext approach suitable for implementation on the World Wide Web.

2. Richardson and Reyes (1995) claim rather better results in their evaluation of two referral systems. However, the systems they dealt with were restricted to government documents, only two searchers were used, and both of these were experienced librarians (the authors).

3. Evaluations of such products showed that they tended to produce very poor search results (Lambert, 1989).

4. A paper by Schultz (1989) is a typical example. Although titled "Designing an expert system to assign Dewey classification numbers to scores," the paper describes an exercise in which a sample of MARC records for scores was examined to determine "feasibility" of classification by computer.

CHAPTER 2

Applications Closely Related to Library Problems

There are a number of applications of intelligent technologies that emanate from outside the information service field but are, nevertheless, highly relevant to information center activities and interests. Applications of this kind fall in such areas as intelligent text processing, intelligent agents, intelligent interfaces, and data mining.

Intelligent text processing[1]

Use of computers to manipulate text in electronic form began in the late 1950s, and the 1960s saw the initiation of an incredible number of research projects in this area. There were several reasons for the explosion of activity: research institutions (and researchers) found themselves with expensive computing facilities that were looking for applications, research funding was generously available from many government sources, and text processing was widely considered to be a rather simple task for computers viewed as "powerful" (getting significant amounts of text into electronic form was usually regarded as a greater obstacle).

While machine translation was the major goal of much of this research, various approaches to information retrieval were also under investigation. The most ambitious projects in information retrieval sought to develop "question-answering" or "fact retrieval" systems—i.e., systems capable of answering a user question directly rather than retrieving a text that may contain the answer or, more commonly, a reference to such a text.

Of course, the problems turned out to be much greater than anticipated, particularly in the area of machine translation. Interest in text processing rapidly began to wane within the research community as well as the funding agencies, although some of the better projects persisted and, over the years, showed considerable improvement and offered promising results.

The breadth of text processing research today is reminiscent of the activity of the 1970s (see Jacobs, 1992c, and Pereira and Grosz, 1994, to get some idea of the present state of the art). This increase in interest and activity stems from the facts that vast quantities of text are now available in electronic form, that computing power is much greater and much cheaper, and that there are now well-recognized needs for viable text processing applications in public and private sectors (e.g., efficient dissemination of information over the Internet and the mandated multilingual requirements of the European Community). Current research seeks to develop "text-based intelligent systems."

Paradoxically, the sheer quantity of text available to be processed today presents significant challenges but also offers potential solutions that were not available to the investigators of 30 years ago. For example, lexicons of word roots or word senses can contain many thousands of entries rather than a few hundred (Jacobs and Rau, 1994) and word associations (co-occurrences) in significant bodies of text can be used to disambiguate words preparatory to the more sophisticated linguistic processing of syntactic analysis (Wilks et al., 1992). Word frequency can also be used to assign text to various categories (Jacobs, 1992b).

In addition, "statistical filtering," based on the co-occurrence of particular words or roots, can be used to select those sentences that seem most likely to be "relevant" to a particular requirement and, thus, the best candidates for more refined analysis (Wilks et al., 1992)

Charniak (1995) has pointed out that 90 percent accuracy can be obtained in assigning a part-of-speech "tag" to a word simply on the basis of the most likely (most frequently occurring) case, and this accuracy can be increased to 95-96 percent by some simple context checks (i.e., looking at adjacent words).

Stanfill and Waltz (1992) compare the approaches of today with those of the earlier years: "AI as it has been formulated in the past is, if not yet dead, dying; a new AI is taking its place. The old AI was based on rules and logic. The new AI is based on statistics—but not statistics as it has been formulated in the past. The practice of statistics itself is undergoing a substantial transformation" (Page 215). Jacobs (1992a) points out that the approaches of today derive "more power from large quantities of stored text than from hand-crafted rules."

Current approaches to text processing can be considered "intelligent" to the extent that computers can be made to "understand" the text.[2] "Understand" here means being able to interpret the meaning of a sentence unambiguously. Normally this requires some form of syntactic analysis. Syntactic analysis seeks to determine the role of a word in a sentence (e.g., noun or verb), to recognize the different structural elements (noun phrase, verb phrase, prepositional phrase, and so on), and thus to determine the various dependencies of a sentence (e.g., subject, subject modifier, object, object modifier).

Intelligent text processing is being used, experimentally or operationally, in a number of applications, including text categorization, text extraction, summarization and augmentation, text generation, and enhanced information retrieval, as well as machine translation.[3]

Text categorization refers to the process of classifying text items— i.e., putting them into particular pre-established categories. For example, the CONSTRUE system, developed for Reuters, Ltd., classifies a stream of news stories using a scheme of up to 674 categories (Hayes, 1992). Chen et al. (1994) describe procedures for identifying concepts occurring in the text of electronic meetings; in this case the concepts are determined by the procedures rather than being pre-established. Yang and Liu (1999) evaluated five text categorization systems based on a diverse set of methods, finding neural networks and a Bayes classifier to be inferior to the other statistical methods studied.

Text extraction can be considered to take text categorization one stage further. The objective is to identify pieces of text (e.g., paragraphs) that deal with a particular topic and to extract them. In some cases, the process goes beyond simple extraction to reduce the text to structured (template filling) form. To take a completely hypothetical example, a system might monitor movement of business executives through analysis of news items, and the sentence "John F. Ritter, vice president of sales at ABC for the past 5 years, has been appointed executive vice president at XYZ" might be reduced to the following structure:

Executive: John F. Ritter
Former position: Vice president of sales
Former employer: ABC
New position: Executive vice president
New employer: XYZ
Date: November 5, 1996 (date of news item)

Cowie and Lehnert (1996) provide a useful overview of the state of the art of text extraction.

There are many potential applications for this type of text extraction and template (frame) filling, perhaps the most obvious being the production of summaries of current news. Haug and Beesley (1992) discuss another application in which data from patient records can be recognized automatically, extracted, and placed under a limited number of headings (e.g., "patient complains of," "patient denies") to aid a radiologist in the interpretation of x-rays. Paice and Jones (1993) discuss the use of a frame-filling approach in the construction of automatic abstracts. Another specialized application of the template approach is the extraction of bibliographic citations from the text of patents (Lawson et al., 1996).

A major ongoing effort in information extraction is the Message Understanding Conference, which is now in its seventh round (MUC-7). Like TREC, this is an ongoing large-scale experiment, with participants from various academic, commercial, and government agencies. Within MUC, information extraction is defined as "the extraction of information from a text in the form of text strings and processed text strings which are placed into slots labeled to indicate the kind of information that can fill them" (Chinchor, 1998). The documents used in these experiments are unstructured texts taken from sources such as the New York Times News Service. The slots that are filled after strings are extracted and processed may "represent an entity with its attributes, a relationship between two or more entities, or an event with various entities playing roles and/or being in certain relationships" (Chinchor, 1998). Results of these experiments are reported as recall and precision values. More information about MUC can be found at its Web site at http://www.muc.saic.com/proceedings_index.html and in a comprehensive paper by Hirschman (1998).

Text linkage uses statistical and/or syntactic analyses to determine similarities between different passages of text, usually from completely different documents, and thereby link them (Salton and Buckley, 1992; Maarek, 1992). In essence, the approach can be applied to produce hypertext links automatically.[4]

Text augmentation can be considered an extension of text linkage. Systems designed for this purpose attempt to integrate pieces of text from several sources into a coherent narrative—e.g., by following news on some event, such as a corporate merger or natural disaster, in newspapers. A variation of this is research to develop tools that integrate text and pictorial input—e.g., relate a descriptive passage in a textbook to elements in a diagram and extract text to elucidate the diagram itself (Rajagopalan, 1994). Chen (1993) describes a computer "model" for the integration of related text from different sources.

Text summarization appears to be the term currently in vogue for what has been known, in the past, as *automatic abstracting* or, more correctly, *automatic extracting*—the automatic selection of sentences from a text to act as a useful summary (abstract). Sentences are selected on the basis of statistical and/or linguistic criteria. While the criteria used today are more sophisticated, they do not differ much in principle from the criteria first used by such investigators as Luhn, Baxendale, and Edmundson in the late 1950s and early 1960s.

Nevertheless, the more sophisticated approaches of today will go beyond the mere selection of sentences—e.g., they may conflate two or more sentences into a single, coherent, nonredundant sentence or they may create simple narrative summaries from discrete items of data.

The state of the art of text summarization of the latter type is exemplified in papers by McKeown et al. (1995) and Maybury (1995). The former generate narrative summaries from stored data (rather than narrative text) relating to basketball games and to telephone network planning activity, while Maybury's system generates textual summaries from highly condensed and structured military messages (battle event data). On the other hand, more traditional techniques, such as conventional IR statistical methods and some linguistic cues, continue to be employed. Goldstein et al. (1999) used such methods in extracting and ranking sentences for inclusion in news article summaries.

The network environment presents new opportunities and challenges for automatic summarization. For example, Hui and Goh (1996) have experimented with the automatic generation of abstracts of newspaper articles as part of a World Wide Web retrieval and filtering interface.

Text generation here refers both to tools that generate limited types of text automatically and expert systems that aid humans in the writing of various types of reports. Systems of the latter type exist, for example, to aid in the generation of product documentation in industry by providing online access to text and graphics that may be repetitively applicable in the creation of various types of reports (see G.L. Smith, 1991, as one example). Mellisch and Dale (1998) describe recent work in text generation and problems associated with evaluating its results. More sophisticated systems are exemplified by the "editor's workbench," described by Bateman and Teich (1995), which will extract text and structure it in response to editorial requirements. Modern "intelligent writing assistants" will do much more than check spelling; they will give advice on word choice and correct grammar and usage (Oakman, 1994).

Several commercial products support various report-writing tasks. One example, Plan Write, from Business Resource Software, is a step-by-step guide to writing a business plan, including checklists, spreadsheets, chart generators, a model plan, and other guides, as well as word processing and spell checking.

Stock (1993) describes an interesting hypermedia system (ALFRESCO) for retrieving images on 14th century Italian frescoes and information concerning them. Among other features, the system incorporates a natural language search interface and the ability to generate coherent answers from "canned texts" associated with different images of frescoes stored within a hypermedia network. Stock gives an example of the question "Can you show and describe to me a fresco by Ambrogio Lorenzetti in Siena?" which could generate the following response:

> The Effects of Good Government is a fresco by
> Ambrogio Lorenzetti in the Public Palace. The Effects

of Good Government was painted in 1338. A fresco
from the same period is S. Silvestro and the Holy
Kings by Maso di Banco, painted in 1330-1340.
Another work by Ambrogio Lorenzetti in a monu-
ment of Siena is the Announcement, of 1344, in the
Pinacoteca.

The various components of this rather complete answer are drawn
from canned texts appearing in different parts of the hypermedia
network.

Dale et al. (1998) describe a text generation system that does not
use a knowledge base and therefore cannot be described as "intelligent." They report on work in progress where they are trying to generate large numbers of texts automatically from a museum database.

A specialized text-generation application has been described by
Demasco and McCoy (1992). They work to develop an interface to
help people with severe motor impairments to compose text. A "virtual keyboard" allows users to select from displays of letters, words,
or phrases, and a semantic parser is then used to generate a "well-
formed sentence." They use the term "sentence compansion" to refer
to this process that could, for example, take the selected words
"John," "study," "weather," "big," and "university" and form a sentence "John studies weather at a big university." The work is still
experimental and, as of 1992, operated with a limited vocabulary of
around 2,000 words.

Kerpedjiev (1992) deals with another specialized text generation
situation. In this case, meteorological data can be used to generate
"multimodal" weather reports; the reports can be in the form of narrative text, maps, tables, or a combination of these, according to the
requirements of the user.

Canned text can also be used to generate the explanations that arc
often considered to be an essential element in the operation of an
expert system (see Lewin, 1992, for an example drawn from medical
informatics).

Information retrieval is implied in all of the text processing activities already mentioned. In terms of sophistication, the retrieval of

sentences or paragraphs falls midway between the retrieval of biblio-
graphical references (typical of most of the online searching performed in libraries) and the retrieval of actual answers to questions.
Enhancements to conventional database searching (e.g., intelligent
interfaces) are dealt with elsewhere in this book. Also dealt with elsewhere, even though it may involve text processing, is information filtering. Croft and Turtle (1992) maintain that significant improvements in information retrieval will require techniques that, in some
sense, "understand" the contents of documents and queries and can
thus infer the probability that an item will be useful.

Machine translation, which is perhaps the most sophisticated
application of text processing, has made considerable progress since
the early work of the 1950s, and many operating systems are now in
existence. Nath (1999) describes the state of the art in this area, noting many trade-offs, such as degree of automation versus accuracy,
and depth versus breadth of processing. For very practical reasons,
the Commission of the European Communities has been a leader in
this area. Despite the progress, however, completely automatic systems—i.e., systems not requiring some human editing of output—
remain "a distant goal" (Hutchins, 1986). Hutchins points out that AI
techniques have had little real impact on machine translation and
that the most successful of current systems contain little "linguistic
sophistication." Nevertheless, he believes that it is realistic to expect
the development of multilingual systems having very large vocabularies, performing at 90 percent accuracy, and operating at a fraction
of the cost of human translation.

One of the oldest and most successful systems, Systran, in some
applications incorporates dictionaries of as many as 350,000 words.
In a Russian-English application, involving translation of nearly
100,000 pages of text, less than 5 percent of output is said to contain
errors (Hutchins and Somers, 1992).

The most ambitious machine translation project, Eurotra, a project of the European Community, has not yet resulted in fully operational systems.

Reviewing the state of the art of machine translation in 1992,
Hutchins and Somers predicted: "... that there will not, in the

foreseeable future, be an 'ideal' system capable of accepting all types of texts in all or most subjects producing output to the standard of the best human translators, and that there will not be MT systems capable of literary translation" (Page 331).

A rather different type of "translation" application involves the conversion of one form of representation to another. The most obvious situation exists in the field of chemistry, where Eggert et al. (1992, 1993) have described an expert system approach to converting chemical formulas to names, and vice versa, and Ibison et al. (1993) have produced a prototype that will scan the image of a chemical structure embedded in a page of text and convert it to a computer-readable (connection table) output.

An area of investigation very much related to machine translation is referred to as Cross Linguistic Information Retrieval (CLIR). Grefenstette (1998) discusses current research and current problems in finding documents in languages other than that of the original query, and surveys approaches for identification of the target language, for automatically generating queries in different languages, and for merging results from disparate sources. Franz and McCarley (1999) proposed the addition of document translation to this scenario, and showed modest improvements in TREC experiments. The MuST project (Lin, 1999) goes further in not only retrieving documents from multilingual databases, but also summarizing and translating the documents into one of several languages; this system is in prototype phase.

Machine translation has also been spotlighted by the Internet in providing access to so many documents in many different languages. AltaVista is making use of Systran to translate documents from English into five other European languages (Banks, 1998), but Watters and Patel (1999) raise questions about the quality of these translations. Another system that claims to be freely available and very useful is Globalink (Lanza, 1998).

The methods used in much of text processing today are not particularly new. Most of them were used, perhaps in a more rudimentary form, 30 or more years ago by Luhn, Baxendale, Edmundson, Borko, Maron, Simmons, Salton and many other investigators. See Chapter

9 of Lancaster (1968b) for an overview of this area in the 1960s. As suggested earlier, better results can be achieved today because much greater bodies of electronic text are now available, and the power of present-day computers allows the processing of such text with reasonable efficiency.

Nevertheless, even the most sophisticated of current methods are far from ideal in terms of results achieved, processing time and processing costs. Moreover, there are still relatively few systems that are truly "operational" in the sense that they provide a real service on an everyday basis.

Jacobs (1992a) sees the situation as follows: "While there has been some visible progress toward text-based intelligent systems, we aren't very close to a desirable state of technology" (Page 5). Hobbs et al. (1992) claim that the ultimate objective is to develop a system that will: "... recover all information that is implicitly or explicitly present in the text, and it should do so without making mistakes. This standard is far beyond the state of the art. It is an impossibly high standard for human beings, let alone machines" (Pages 13-14).

McDonald (1992) points out that, in general, the best of modern parsers can only deal with relatively short and simple sentences. For longer and more complex sentences, the best they can do is identify component fragments (e.g., noun phrases); they are far from being able to produce a complete, unambiguous analysis. For a typical newspaper-length sentence of 20-25 words, current parsers could potentially come up with hundreds of possible analyses. In McDonald's words, "no parser even comes close to understanding everything in a real text, such as a news article."

Even with relatively small corpora (around 1,500 messages) of short texts (typically around 14 sentences), the best of current methods are far from producing perfect results—e.g., in a text extraction exercise, not all relevant sentences are selected and not all selected sentences are relevant. Under controlled evaluation conditions, the best of current techniques operate at around the 50-50 mark (Jacobs and Rau, 1994; Sundheim, 1995)—e.g., they produce about half the templates (structured representations based on text extracted from the messages) they should produce, and about half those produced are wanted (i.e., match the pre-established standard).[5] While some text processing systems report much better results, they do so for much simpler tasks. For example, Hayes (1992) reports 94 percent recall and 84 percent precision for CONSTRUE but the task performed—putting news items into up to 200 categories—is simpler than the text extraction/template filling tasks.

Under controlled conditions, much better scores can be obtained in simpler extraction tasks (e.g., finding named entities in text) or simpler template filling tasks—involving extraction of text related to named entities (Sundheim, 1995; Chinchor, 1998).

The 50-50 level of performance in sentence extraction/template completion needs also to be put into context. These results are achieved in very limited domains (e.g., terrorist activity in Latin America). To achieve the sentence selection, a domain-specific dictionary must be created. Even in a very limited domain, this can be labor-intensive (1,500 person hours quoted for one), although tools have been developed to construct such dictionaries automatically or semi-automatically (see Riloff and Lehnert, 1993, for an example).[6]

Current approaches to producing "intelligent" summaries (automatic abstracts) of documents are also unimpressive. The system developed by Brandow et al. (1995), and evaluated by them, produced summaries that were judged significantly less acceptable than "leading text." What this means is that human analysts, on the average, judge, say, the first 250 words of a text to be a better indicator of its content than a 250-word abstract composed of sentences selected from the text automatically.

Development of the limited systems in existence is very expensive. CONSTRUE, for example, required 9.5 person years of effort (Hayes and Weinstein, 1991).

It is interesting to note that the 50-50 type of results reported for modern text processing systems are very close to the performance level reported for large bibliographic retrieval systems (e.g., MEDLARS) in the 1960s (Lancaster, 1968a). While on the surface the comparison seems unfair, since the text extraction/template filling tasks are clearly more complex than the reference retrieval task, it must also be recognized that the corpora used in the more sophisticated tasks are trivially small compared with the size of the bibliographic databases of even 30 years ago (roughly 1,500 messages versus half a million bibliographic records).[7]

The fact is that the relatively crude Boolean search methods most commonly used to search large bibliographic databases today, despite their many critics, produce remarkably good results considering the size of the corpora dealt with, a point made very cogently by Stanfill and Waltz (1992): "The surprising thing (from the point of view of AI) is that the statistical approach, using no domain-specific knowledge at all, works. And it works for quantities of information (gigabytes) that are unimaginably large by the standards of AI" (Page 217). Note that they were referring to simple Boolean search approaches as used in indexed (e.g., MEDLINE) or full text (e.g., NEXIS) databases and not the more sophisticated ranked output approaches.

Jacobs (1992a) has identified several challenges facing researchers in the area of text processing today: making systems more robust (greater accuracy, faster, cheaper in linguistic analysis), refining capabilities (e.g., going from document retrieval to passage retrieval to answer retrieval), and making output more cost-effective or attractive to the user (by highlighting, text extraction, or summarization).

Although these general assertions about the performance and state of the art of intelligent text processing systems were made several years ago, they continue to be valid today. In fact, text processing has followed a general trend of using more and more surface-oriented (lexical, morphological, and at most syntactic) techniques combined with statistics to process the large bodies of text that are now available; this has been true of both standalone systems and those available through the Internet. Indeed, Internet text processing within the search domains is an application of many long-standing IR techniques, and their automatic categorization techniques also make extensive use of statistics and user-defined roles for terms (a more machine-aided approach, in fact), and cannot thus be considered "intelligent."

As of the mid-1990s, there were several automatic text processing systems in full operation. Of particular note was CONSTRUE, developed by the Carnegie Group for Reuters, Ltd. (Hayes and Weinstein,

1991; Hayes, 1992). It was fairly successful in the limited classification task (putting news stories into up to 200 categories) it was designed for. Although costly to develop (9.5 person years), the system replaced several human indexers. Its use was estimated to reduce costs at Reuters by $752,000 in 1990 and expected to reduce them by $1,264,000 in 1991. More rapid processing[8] and more consistent processing were also claimed.

The software developed for Reuters was generalized into a commercial product, Text Categorization Shell (TCS), operating on up to 674 categories. TCS was also being used in a classified government application involving routing of messages to intelligence analysts. In this case, only five categories were involved (Hayes, 1992).

A system somewhat similar to CONSTRUE was described by Goodman (1991). Known as Prism, and developed by Cognitive Systems Inc., it was used by large banks to route telex messages to appropriate departments. It would assign to over 100 categories and also had the ability to extract selectively from the message texts.

Another Carnegie product, Name Finder, looked for personal and corporate names in news feeds in order to provide an alerting service based on names of interest. The product was intelligent to the extent that it had built-in rules capable of recognizing acceptable variants of corporate and other names (Hayes and Koerner, 1993).

Also developed for Reuters by the same company, Carnegie Group, Inc., was a fact extraction system, JASPER (Journalist's Assistant for Preparing Earnings Reports). Working with an electronic stream of company press releases, the system would identify messages that contained earnings and dividend information, extract various facts (e.g., net income, per share income) and place these into a template (Andersen et al., 1992). Hayes (1992) referred to this as a "candidate" news story that could be routed to a journalist for validation or editing.

Text generation products were exemplified by such products as Spotlight and the Intelligent Correspondence Generator. Spotlight, developed by A. C. Nielsen Co., operated on point-of-sale data to generate status reports on the performance of selected products (e.g., gains/losses in comparison with competitors in various markets, and best-performing and worst-performing markets). The stylized reports were produced on the basis of rules capable of producing a variety of sentences that described the performance of the product, explained the performance, and so on. The rules could also generate tables and graphs. The 200 parameterized rules could generate 70 different sentence types, 10 different graph types, and 10 different table types (Anand and Kahn, 1992, 1993). This system appears to be still in use today.

Springer et al. (1991) described the use of the Intelligent Correspondence Generator (ICG), a product of Cognitive Systems, at a credit card company. In this application, customer service representatives used the ICG to generate customized letters based on data drawn from a client database and from the representative's own input. The system used over 100 composition templates and almost 900 rules. The templates could be nested in various ways to produce the letter needed for the case in hand. The application was said to improve quality of correspondence and reduce costs. Turnaround time for letter generation was reduced from days to minutes.

Software for text generation was commercially available from several sources. In some cases, the software was specifically promoted for particular applications. To give just one example, Knowledge Point focused on the area of human resource management, producing software that could help the manager create job descriptions, employee reviews, employee handbooks, and similar products. The software gave the manager various forms of online help and advice in these tasks, as well as in generating appropriate text.

Of all the text processing systems, the most widely used were those devoted to machine translation. Hutchins and Somers (1992) surveyed a wide range of applications in government and industry. Xerox, for example, used Systran to translate technical manuals (about 60,000 pages a year) into French, German, Spanish, Italian, and Portuguese. Systran continues to be a viable product as evidenced by its use with the AltaVista Web search engine (Banks, 1998).

A useful summary of commercial applications of text processing as of the mid-1990s can be found in Church and Rau (1995); they also discuss prospects for the future in various processing areas. Since the reports of the systems developed by the Carnegie Group and

Cognitive Systems, Inc. were published in the mid-1990s, much has happened to change both the markets and the applications for this type of software. The Carnegie Group has ceased its offerings of Text Categorization Shell, Name Finder, and JASPER, since, according to a company representative, the market for these products is no longer viable; the Carnegie Group has since merged with Logica, Inc. and is now out of the text processing market entirely. Cognitive Systems ceased trading in 1996 and no one could be reached for further information on their products.

Some commercial applications do remain in the text processing arena. One of these is CLARIT (http://www.clarit.com), which provides a suite of programs that can automatically route and tag, summarize, and cluster documents, as well as provide advanced statistical search and retrieval operations. CLARIT has taken part in the ongoing TREC evaluation, and has performed as well or better than other systems in those experiments.

Another product that can be searched by subscription through a Web browser is DR-LINK. The product began as an NLP-based search and retrieval tool developed and marketed by TextWise, Inc. (Liddy, 1998). It has since been acquired by Mann & Napier, and now has a suite of visualization and data mining tools added to its capabilities (http://www.mnis.net/dr_link.htm).

A new market has emerged for text processing software because of the burgeoning Internet/intranet market. There are now many products described on the Web and elsewhere that serve many of the same functions as the systems previously described, but now within a distributed information environment.

In the beginning of the Internet, when there were few documents available and hypertext browsing was a novelty, no one saw the need for large-scale text-processing applications. However, as the Web grew, it became increasingly obvious that tools had to be developed to search for specific information. Search engines, exemplified by Lycos and its free text statistical ranking on the one hand, and Yahoo! and its human derived and applied categorization scheme on the other, were developed.

As the Web has grown ever larger, a phenomenon has occurred that has been known for some time within the IR community (Blair and Maron, 1985). As information retrieval systems based on crude automatic text processing techniques grow larger, their performance measured by recall and precision degrades. Hence, within the Web software development community, there have been increasing numbers of products that attempt to provide more sophisticated text processing, including categorization, summarization, and translation software. Some representative Web machine translation systems have already been described.

Extractor, a system developed through the National Research Council of Canada, claims to be a text summarization system that works with English, French, German, and Japanese documents and can be integrated into a Web browser. Although it is still evolving as a product, it appears that at present it is more of a text extractor than a text summarization system, since it can extract key phrases and key sentences from unstructured text, which constitutes a "mini-summary" of the document. Further details and a demonstration of the software's capabilities can be found at http://ii145.ai.iit.nrc.ca.

A larger market within the Internet/intranet community is for text categorization software, which can either be integrated into the user's Web browser to search and retrieve information available publicly, or to provide more sophisticated organization and retrieval capabilities for a given company's documents housed on its intranet. These products include Autonomy (http://www.autonomy.com/tech/index.html); Verity (http://www.verity.com/products/index.html); and UltraSeek (http://www.ultraseek.com/products/products.htm), a product of InfoSeek. In some cases, such as with Autonomy, the categorization method is referred to as "unsupervised," which means that the categorization algorithm, based in their case on neural network technology, makes use of only a body of text provided by the user. In the case of UltraSeek, however, the categorization method is "supervised," which refers to the need to provide a local thesaurus and indexing rules that the software can use for its application to the collection.

Intelligent agents

Blake (1994) has defined "information agent" as "software that can retrieve data intelligently from multiple information sources without any human intervention." This section of the book looks at the present status of "intelligent" agents of this type. Useful reviews of the characteristics and state of the art of such agents can be found in Roesler and Hawkins (1994), Feldman and Yu (1999), and Coult (1999).

The term "intelligent agent" has been applied to tools capable of performing various information retrieval-type tasks within the Internet and also to tools designed to achieve more specialized goals in smaller universes of data—e.g., personnel databases and other resources within a corporation.

Uses of the second type of agent have been reviewed by Blanchard (1996) and a rather complete survey of all types can be found in Mendes et al. (1996). A typical business application is personnel review; within a large organization an agent can track employee review dates and automatically initiate the review process by transmitting the necessary forms, through fax or e-mail, to the appropriate supervisor. Other agents operate in the areas of customer service, manufacturing, and retail sales. One customer service application occurs in banking where agents can look up an account number, verify customer identity, and read various items of information from fields on a screen. Agents can also monitor an account and inform a customer—by fax, telephone, or paper—if balance drops below a specified amount. Another agent that is becoming increasingly common is one that assists with the scheduling of meetings based on information on the availabilities, behavior, and preferences of the people involved (Maes, 1994). Bocionek (1995) describes and discusses the learning capabilities of two office automation agents (for calendar management and for room management). Nardi et al. (1998) describe Apple Data Detectors, a system that extracts structure and semantics from documents automatically without requiring users to create documents in new ways.

McKenna (1999) analyzes two pieces of software that incorporate agent technology: British Telcom's Knowledge Management, tools that are used to create "shared knowledge spaces," and Orbital

Software's Organik suite, in which agents build statistical models of personal interests and expertise that are then used to match people having similar interests.

However, it is the Internet-related agents that are of more interest to the information science community. New Internet-related software products are emerging on a regular basis so it is difficult to keep up with these technologies. Because of very rapid changes, our discussion deals with capabilities rather than individual products. While a few commercial products are mentioned, they are included for illustrative purposes only and represent only a fraction of those available. Product descriptions undoubtedly promise more than they can deliver, so one can only gauge their true capabilities by trying them out. Several useful reviews of the current capabilities and challenges of agent technology in the distributed information environment can be found in the literature (Haverkamp and Gauch, 1998; Murugesan, 1998; and Bradley, 1999).

The Web search engines themselves have little in the way of intelligent features. Although they may rank output, the ranking is usually based only on the frequency of occurrence of words in Web pages or other sources searched or on the number of the search words occurring in the source (assuming a search input as a natural language statement). Other factors that may be taken into account in ranking include the place in which search words occur in the source, their proximity in the source, and/or the number of pages they point to and/or that point to them. Some do claim to link synonymous terms so that "concept" rather than "word" search is performed, but it is difficult to discover how well this is achieved. Some search engines operate on complete text while others create various forms of condensation based on extracting parts of the text (e.g., the first X words) and/or extracting high-frequency words.

Excite is a search engine that claims more sophisticated features, including "query by example" (looking for items "like" one already judged useful) and the ability to extract relevant sentences from retrieved items. This engine also claims a more powerful and sophisticated search technology, known as Intelligent Concept Extraction, which is "able to find and score documents based on a correlation of their concepts, as well as actual keywords" but the algorithm is proprietary and, thus, it is difficult to know how it operates. Moreover, one evaluation (Venditto, 1996) showed little difference between this and keyword search. The metasearch engines (which search across several other search engines) may also claim "intelligent" features, such as elimination of duplicates and "keeping watch" to update a standing search. Savvy Search will rank search engines according to probability of value in satisfying a particular query; it claims to use its own past experience, as well as the query terms, in this, but it is not clear what the other ranking factors are (Howe and Dreilinger, 1997). Scales and Felt (1995), Conte (1996), Kimmel (1996), Venditto (1996), Pfaffenberger (1996), Chu and Rosenthal (1996), Ding and Marchionini (1996), Watson et al. (1996), Nicholson (1997) and Dong and Su (1997) have published useful reviews of search engine capabilities but these change so rapidly that any published account is already somewhat out of date when it appears. More up-to-date information can be found at Search Engine Watch, a Web site at http://searchenginewatch.com (Feldman, 1997).

Software is now available, commercially or at least on an experimental basis, to perform a variety of tasks related to Internet resources, including:

1. Looking for a product (e.g., a CD) at the cheapest price (Perkowitz et al., 1997)

2. Filtering e-mail messages according to pre-established user criteria, including prioritizing some, deleting others, and putting retained messages into selected categories ("folders")

3. Filtering out unwanted Internet advertising and other items that may be unwanted, including those that may be judged unsuitable for access by children[9]

4. Monitoring selected network sources and informing the user when a particular condition is met (e.g., a stock price drops to a certain level) or merely when the source has been updated;

in some cases, the agent will retrieve the change or new information and bring it to the user's attention

5.   Expanding a search query by finding terms that are synonymous or nearly synonymous to the user's initial terms

6.   "Pushing" news items (or other types of information) to network users within selected categories (e.g., sports scores, financial news); some products of this kind are designed as filtering agents to "feed" corporate intranets (Rapoza, 1996a); McCleary (1994) reviewed services of this kind, but her survey is now getting rather old

7.   Searching across multiple Internet sources or disparate sources within an enterprise's own intranet[10]

8.   Bringing forms of entertainment (films, CDs, books) to a person's attention based on a profile of interest (which may be in the form of terms and/or other items known to have been selected in the past)

9.   "Data mining" across the Internet (see next section of the book)[11]

10.   Indexing a local database maintained on a Web server; tools of this kind may have limited "intelligent text" capabilities (Richardson, 1996)

11.   Creating a kind of user profile that is then used to inform the user of sources of interest (Khan et al., 1997) often by classifying and/or filtering documents (Khan and Card, 1997; Kurzke et al., 1998; Krulwich and Burkey, 1997). Tegenbos and Nieuwenhuysen (1997) describe the capabilities of Autonomy, a commercial product that purports to have intelligent agent search capabilities.

Agents designed to customize news delivery via the Internet have been reviewed by Holzberg (1996) and other network-related agents by Griswold (1996). However, changes occur so rapidly that published surveys are at least partly outdated by the time they appear.

In general, most of these tools fall nicely into the categories "watchers," "searchers," and "analysts" (Blake, 1994). Most would qualify as spiders, which Eichmann (1995) has defined as "a program that autonomously explores the structure of the Web and takes some action upon the artifacts thereby encountered." Other terms occurring in the literature include "knowbot" and "softbot." The latter is simply a generic term for software agents in general ("software robots") while the former has been used to refer to agents capable of searching over a number of different information sources (Roesler and Hawkins, 1994). An excellent review of present capabilities for agents of the type listed earlier (but not a critique of commercial software) can be found in Maes (1994).

These various tools can be considered "intelligent" in that some of them at least have a limited learning capability. For example, a user interest profile for a news filtering service can be modified on the basis of user feedback in the form of items selected or rejected. The same principle would apply to an entertainment selection agent. Learning aspects of agents, based on a meetings scheduler, are discussed by Mitchell et al. (1994), while Selker (1994) discusses learning features of a teaching agent.

Resnick and Varian (1997) have compiled a group of articles that deal with "recommender systems." Systems of this type involve "collaborative filtering"—within the Internet, for example, the recommendations of individuals are aggregated and made available to any potential user. Recommendations can relate to any type of Web resource, including even individual messages.

Web-based agents are not necessarily free from problems. For example, they can generate substantial extra loads on servers that may already be overloaded. Also, some sites have already begun to block access by agents. Eichmann (1995) has discussed such problems and proposed an "ethic" for the use of agents within the Web. Although not specifically touched upon by Eichmann, other possible problems may emerge from the use of agents. For example, if an agent is responsible for breach of copyright, is the user legally responsible? Is the manufacturer?

Ordille (1996) points out that agents roaming the Internet can threaten a server with theft of assets, system resources, and reputation. Less widely recognized is the fact that servers can threaten roaming agents in exactly the same way.[12]

Work to produce better Internet-related processing tools continues in the research setting. One system of particular interest, FAQ Finder, was developed at the University of Chicago. FAQ Finder is a question-answering system based on the files of "frequently asked questions" associated with many Usenet newsgroups. In response to a user's question, which can be stated in natural language form, FAQ Finder will first find the FAQ file most likely to yield the answer and then search this file to find the most likely answer. The best match is achieved through a form of syntactic analysis and through use of the WordNet[13] database to find synonymous or nearly synonymous expressions (Hammond et al., 1995; Burke et al., 1997).

Other research groups are working on different aspects of Internet searching. For example, Desai (1997) suggests a metadata search approach based on a "semantic header" database. The Digital Library Initiative at the University of Illinois has been studying methods of searching across several distributed text repositories, including the possibility of switching automatically from one technical vocabulary to another (Schatz et al., 1996). Related work, performed at the University of Arizona, is investigating a graphic (map-like) approach to browsing the Internet (Chen et al., 1995, 1996, 1998b) and an intelligent agent ("personal spider") that, given a home page that is known to be of interest, will find other home pages that are similar (Chen et al., 1998a, 1998d). Pazzani et al. (1995) describe work to develop a filtering and searching agent that will learn from "hotlists" and "coldlists" (items selected as interesting or not interesting by a user). Eberts and Habibi (1995) report that agents based on neural net technology have better learning capabilities than those that are rule-based; they describe three experimental systems. Croi et al. (1999) also applied neural nets in agent development.

Research to develop more intelligent interfaces to the Internet proceeds at the University of Washington (Etzioni and Weld, 1994), and a major center for research on intelligent information processing agents of all types remains the MIT Media Laboratory (Maes, 1994). Work is also being done on software tools to allow network users to develop their own agents (see Thomas, 1995, as an example) or to build their own catalogs of the contents of selected servers (Joy, 1996).[14] Other groups are working on a related but much more difficult problem: agents for filtering and designing customized feeds from television broadcasting (Kim et al., 1996). It is much more difficult because it is ultimately dependent on technologies (speech recognition, natural language understanding, vision processing, machine learning) that are still very immature.

For a broad overview of intelligent agents, covering the whole range of possibilities from local agents to mobile agents, a conference paper by Magedanz et al. (1996) can be strongly recommended.

Indermaur (1995) concludes his review of intelligent agents by suggesting that the field is still in its infancy and that it "will take more development work to produce wide scale commercial applications." He goes on to say: "We have not created the general-purpose, intelligent agents of our imaginations, but we have taken the crucial first steps. Agents will someday make it possible for software to 'do what I mean, not what I say'" (Page 104).

While Indermaur is correct in his belief that the field has a long way to go, he may be overly optimistic on what can be achieved. Others make more modest claims. For example, Blake (1994) quotes one software executive (from SandPoint, which produced the Hoover search engine) as follows:

> Michael Kinkead, President of SandPoint, is quick to emphasise that Hoover is not intended as a substitute for a trained information professional, nor does he feel that information agents necessarily represent the next generation of online services: 'There will always be searches which need a human brain between each iteration to define the terms and strategy. What

Hoover does is perform clerical searching tasks where all the intelligence can be built into the search engine and a human mind is not needed.

'The information staff employed by our clients tell us that, once casual corporate users start discovering what kind of external information they can retrieve, the number of search requests they get actually goes up— because this new group of users soon starts after needing complex searches that Hoover cannot tackle' (Page 189).

Intelligent interfaces

Equipping a system with an intelligent interface allows it to be accessed by a wider range of users. Although such interfaces could be used in a variety of application domains, those of most interest for this book are designed to simplify access to information retrieval (IR) systems. The most basic of such interfaces embed some knowledge of databases and systems so that the user need not be familiar with these details in order to retrieve relevant records successfully. More sophisticated interfaces have a user-modeling capability that allows them to adjust to a user's skills and patterns of usage. Vickery and Vickery (1992) offer the following list of functions that an intelligent interface should support:

1. Interact with the user via an easy-to-use interface

2. Tailor its actions to individual user capabilities and preferences

3. Provide screen dialogue in the user's preferred language

4. Undertake linguistic analysis of user queries

5. Give aid in the user selection of database(s) and host(s)

6. Prompt the user in the clarification of queries

7. Transform automatically clarified queries into search statements in the form required by the host/database to be accessed

8. Perform automatically the telecommunication functions of dial-up, logon, and so on

9. Transmit automatically search statements to the host, and download search output

10. Provide means for the user to evaluate search output

11. Give aid to the user in reformulating queries and/or search statements

12. Provide means for the user to order documents online

13. Provide possibilities for post-processing of downloaded search output, in particular the relevance ranking of items.

Vickery (1992) emphasizes that, in a European context, a further important function of the interface is to aid the user whose natural language is not that of the database.

The number, diversity, and scatter of information sources and systems now available in electronic form challenge the ability of non-expert searchers to make effective use of these resources. Databases now may contain bibliographic records, full texts, numeric data, images, or combinations of these types. The retrieval systems on which they are mounted are diverse, with differing interfaces and means of query formulation. The Internet provides the potential for access to retrieval systems and Web sites throughout the world. Stern (1997) notes that the optimal end-user system would provide a platform-independent, less confusing array of options and interfaces, seamlessly connected to a broad-based data delivery system. He cites the Astrophysics Data System sponsored by NASA as an example of a niche-specific integrated system providing access to data from both nonbibliographic and traditional citation sources.

In information retrieval, intelligent interfaces have been termed "front-ends," "intermediary systems," and "gateways." Drenth et al. (1991) and Efthimiadis (1991) provide extensive references to prior work. Tools aiding in database selection were discussed earlier in this book. Intelligent interfaces for retrieval systems may also offer assistance with query definition, search strategy formulation, and search revision.

A number of dimensions are useful in distinguishing among the efforts to provide computer-based assistance to users of retrieval systems via intelligent interfaces:

1.　*Resources accessible via the interface.* The interface is the user's "window" on the world of information available online. It may be highly specialized, intended to help the user in answering a particular type of question. In this case it may link to a single database on a single system and focus on only a part of its contents (e.g., locating literature on particular cancer therapies in a database like MEDLINE). A slightly more general interface would support full use of a single database on a single system. Increased accessibility would be provided by interfaces linking to multiple databases on a single system, and finally to multiple databases on multiple systems.

2.　*Location of the interface.* The interface must be located somewhere between the user and the system(s) being accessed. Possible locations include the user's workstation, on another computer on the network, or on the host system itself.

3.　*Types of assistance provided by the interface.* For the information retrieval task, an interface may provide assistance in query definition (concept identification), database selection (identification of databases to be searched and the systems where they reside), search strategy formulation (selection of terms and modes of combination), and search revision (broadening, narrowing, or other modifications in strategy). In practice, not all of these forms of assistance may be provided by a single interface. Going beyond information retrieval, an interface may also support post-processing functions, ranging from formatting records for easier reading to performing statistical analyses on the content of records. The interface may assist with both clerical and intellectual tasks, with clerical tasks being the easier to automate. Pollitt (1990) suggests four categories of knowledge that need to be incorporated in interfaces to provide assistance with the various search tasks: (1) system (the command language and facilities available in the search system), (2) searching (strategy and tactics to be employed in searching), (3) subject, and (4) user (knowledge about each individual user). Often there is a tradeoff, with some interfaces having general knowledge to support searches of multiple databases on multiple systems while others have in-depth knowledge to support specific categories of questions and/or databases.

4. *Nature of assistance provided by the interface.* The interface may function in two different modes: computer-assisted vs. computer-delegated. In computer-assisted mode, the interface provides advice to the user in making decisions. In computer-delegated mode, the interface makes decisions automatically, given some initial input from the user. Buckland and Florian (1991) suggest that a computer-assisted approach is likely to be more effective because the intelligence of the system and the intelligence of the user ought to augment each other. Bates (1990) has also identified the need to provide optimal combinations of searcher control and system retrieval power, arguing that many users would not want to delegate the entire search process to the interface.

5. *User modeling capabilities.* While the term "user model" emphasizes information about the person using the system, situational, task, or environmental information may also be encoded in the model (Allen, 1990). In intelligent interfaces, user models could be employed to adapt explanations to the user's level of expertise as well as to adapt to user preferences. Brajnik et al. (1990) point out that information about the user

may be obtained through: external acquisition (information is obtained in response to questions posed by the interface) or internal derivation (information about the user is obtained through inference from the search session). Borgman and Plute (1992) call these forms of models stated vs. inferred. Chandler et al. (1997) describe a system that includes a model of a librarian's behavior.

Interface design can take advantage of systematic study of searcher expertise. Inexperienced users are frequently confronted with strategies that retrieve nothing or that retrieve very large sets. Prabha (1991) reviews a number of strategies for reducing large sets. Morris et al. (1989) and Shute and Smith (1993) are examples of researchers who studied human intermediaries' actual search techniques as a basis for designing prototype expert systems to aid in search strategy development. Nardi and O'Day (1996) focus on the expertise involved in communicating with clients and in technical competence in searching. They emphasize the user modeling that occurs, as demonstrated in the extent to which librarians personalize a search with respect to the client's specific ongoing activity. As human searching expertise is better understood, the problem of knowledge acquisition by the interface remains. If performance of interfaces is to improve over time, then some provision for modification or learning must be implemented.

Much of the effort to date has focused on creating interfaces to handle query formulation for multiple bibliographic databases. Poo et al. (2000) report on the E-Reference, which they describe as "an expert system Web interface to online catalogs." Its interface has a set of heuristics that it uses to formulate and reformulate search strategies, and uses the Z39.50 protocol to access online catalogs on the Internet. An initial prototype has been developed and a preliminary evaluation was carried out using 12 queries; results showed that overall it performed better than a non-expert system used for comparison, but worse than a search by a trained librarian.

Another application, called the Selection Recognition Agent (SRA) (Pandit and Kalbag, 1998), uses several modules in a Windows-based application to recognize geographic names, dates, e-mail addresses, phone numbers, Usenet newsgroup names and URLs, as well as a general module for recognizing meaningful words and phrases in text. They evaluated their system, in which known items were being searched for, in terms of numbers of keystrokes and mouse clicks, as well as length of time spent on each task, and found that their system decreased the amount of time and effort required.

As Järvelin (1989) points out, there is also a need for assisting with access to multiple numerical and other types of nonbibliographic databases. While some of the interface functions would correspond to forms of assistance needed for accessing bibliographic databases, others, such as data conversion between varying data representations, must be dealt with in accessing numeric databases.

Tseng (1992) notes that the majority of intelligent interface projects for IR have led to the development of research prototypes or to local systems for particular organizations. Very few have subsequently appeared in the wider public domain, and then with little commercial success. She attributes this to the fact that substantial. improvements in usability of online systems have been made by conventional interface technology, which may be developed far more cheaply than expert systems using large knowledge bases and sophisticated inference engines.

One way that online systems are providing the graphical user interfaces (GUIs) and better help functions that searchers now expect is to require use of a proprietary front-end software package to access their system (Tenopir, 1996). Head (1997) suggests that a well-designed GUI should have the following functional components: multiple windows that can be open simultaneously for multitasking, icons that allow for direct manipulation, navigation by pointing or clicking with a mouse, and consistency across applications that ensures reusability and fluency in future versions. From a cognitive standpoint, GUIs have design components that foster acceptance: providing multiple methods for completing the same task; revealing commands and menu options as needed; using icons that rely on users' recognition of real world objects; creating visual, auditory, or tactile feedback; and enhancing screen visuals with color, font, shape, arrangement, and contrast.

A recent development in the interface research domain has been in the arena of visualization. Fox et al. (1999) describe SENTINEL, which is an information retrieval system based on a variety of techniques, such as the vector space model and neural networks, and which also incorporates a module that presents a three-dimensional visualization of the documents retrieved.

Lin (1997) investigates the utility of "map displays" for information retrieval, noting their ability to convey a large amount of information in a limited space and their usefulness in depicting semantic relationships among terms and documents. The specific display reported on used neural network technology to show complex relationships among documents.

As Denning and Smith (1994) note, merely including the appropriate functionality within an IR system does not ensure that users will effectively take advantage of it. In order to develop a system that is useful, it is important to represent the system's capabilities in a manner that is both convenient and usable. They suggest four design concepts: 1) help the user develop an appropriate conceptual model of the system; 2) provide assistance to the user so that he can map his knowledge of the topic into the system; 3) actively help users explore topic areas; and 4) accommodate different styles of interaction.

Front-end packages reside on the searcher's workstation and handle not only the telecommunications functions but also "know" something about the system to which they are connecting. Examples include SciFinder from Chemical Abstracts Service (Williams, 1995) and Grateful Med (Tilson and East, 1994) from the National Library of Medicine. The successful front-ends are mostly created and maintained by the host online system, have an end-user market in addition to the professional market, and maintain or increase the capabilities of the system, while at the same time making it easier to search. Now a growing number of vendors are offering software for workstations to query multiple Internet search engines simultaneously and allow the user to sort results, remove duplicates, and verify the availability of the links (Notess, 1997). Some commercial online systems now support access via World Wide Web interfaces, but sophisticated search features may be sacrificed.

Intelligent interfaces are designed as tools for users. To assess their performance and to identify areas in need of improvement, it is necessary to evaluate them. For those decisions that are computer-assisted, one must determine if the advice is helpful. For those decisions that are computer-delegated, one must determine if the computer's decisions are appropriate. Where assistance is not offered, one must determine if the targeted user group has the necessary expertise to function unassisted. Because information retrieval is a complex task, it is difficult to develop interfaces that allow inexperienced users to achieve expert levels of performance. One example can be used to illustrate the difficulties that interface designers face in trying to simplify the user's task. An early version of Grateful Med, an interface for the National Library of Medicine's search system, allowed the user to type in author names as initials followed by the surname. The interface then translated this into the form required to search the MED-LINE database, i.e., surname followed by a space and then the initials. Initially Grateful Med did not properly handle some input names. Entering "D.A.B. Lindberg" resulted in the translated string "B. Lindberg DA" because the interface did not expect more than two initials prior to the surname. Clearly this is an error, but the user did not have a way to override this error. Given the possibility of such errors or poor advice in interfaces, systematic evaluation is needed to characterize their strengths and weaknesses and to pinpoint areas in need of improvement.

In defining strategic directions in human-computer interaction research, Myers et al. (1996) highlight universal access to large and complex distributed information systems as a major challenge to interface design. The potential user community of database and other information systems is becoming large and rather nontechnical, with most users likely to remain permanent novices with respect to many of the diverse information sources they can access. It is therefore necessary to develop interfaces that require minimal technical sophistication and expertise by the users but that support a wide variety of information-intensive tasks. Their "wish list" for research and development includes:

> Information-access interfaces must offer great flexibility on how queries are expressed and how data are visualized; they must be able to deal with several kinds of data, for example, multimedia, free text, documents, the Web itself; and they must permit several new styles of interaction beyond the typical, two-step query-specification/result-visualization loop, for example, data browsing, filtering, and dynamic incremental querying. ... Fundamental issues for the future include how best to array tasks between people and computers, create systems that adapt to different kinds of users, and support the changing context of tasks (Page 800).

Data mining and knowledge discovery

"Data mining" and its close relative known as "knowledge discovery" are terms that have come into use only very recently. Trybula (1997) reviews the state of the art in research and application in these areas. He defines data mining as "the basic process employed to analyze patterns in data and extract information," while knowledge discovery is a more sophisticated process in which data are transformed "into previously unknown or unsuspected relationships that can be employed as predictors of future actions." He divides this software into two categories according to whether it operates on numeric or textual databases, and describes the processes of data acquisition and mining/discovery. Saarenvirta (1998) provides a review of data mining from the perspective of improving company profitability, either by reducing costs or increasing revenue, and surveys the various steps in carrying out the data mining process and the various statistical analyses employed. Banerjee (1998) provides another overview, specifically from the perspective of the viability of data mining for libraries.

Mena (1996) lists 20 companies that claim to produce "automatic data mining tools," and new products of this type are appearing on a regular basis. Data mining tools are designed to find "hidden" information in databases comprised of various forms of "hard" (e.g., sales and other financial records) data.[15] The claim is that software of this type can find "patterns" in the data without being specifically requested to do so—i.e., prior hypotheses are not being tested, so the mining of the data can be considered to be initiated by the software itself. (Greene and Hield, 1992, distinguish between "supervised" and "unsupervised" data exploration.) To take a completely hypothetical and simplistic example, the patient records in a hospital might be "mined" to discover that individuals treated for condition X were more likely to recover quickly if they fell into a particular dietary class (were vegetarians, drank wine regularly, or whatever).

Several data mining products are commercially available. One, Knowledge Seeker (from Angoss Software), has been used in a wide variety of marketing, medical, quality control, and other applications (http://www.angoss.com). While some data mining products are application-specific, others are more general. For example, Brachman et al. (1996) refer to one, Clementine (http://www.clear-soft.com), as "widely used without customization…made possible by a highly graphical user interface to data mining functions." Many of the other tools, however, require special training in use and some customization.[16]

An early business system was Spotlight, developed by the A. C. Nielsen Company for analyzing patterns in point-of-sale data—e.g., to find the characteristics of communities in which a particular product sells well (Anand and Kahn, 1992, 1993). Spotlight was developed further into a product called Opportunity Explorer.

Rapaport (1995) discusses "target marketing" applications—e.g., the analysis of demographic data associated with ZIP codes to identify promising audiences for direct mailing—and mentions relevant software. A neural network approach is described by Zahavi and Levin (1995). Matsumoto (1998) provides a brief account of a data mining tool under development in the field of agriculture.

The need for data mining tools arises from the fact that organizations of all kinds now store vast quantities of data by virtue of the fact that it is easy to do so. The characteristics and variety of data mining algorithms are discussed by Fayyad et al. (1996) who also point out that data mining is still in its infancy. Etzioni (1996) discusses the feasibility of applying data mining techniques to the World Wide Web, and Kranakis et al. (1996) discuss the cost-effectiveness aspects (although they deal more with information retrieval in general than data mining in particular).

Edelstein (1996) gives a useful summary of the principles upon which data mining can work (association, sequence, classification, clustering, and forecasting) as well as the types of tools (neural networks, decision trees, rule induction, data visualization) that can be applied to the data mining task. Vickery (1997) reviews the subject from an information science perspective. A directory of data mining products available early in 1996 can be found in Delmonico (1996); Watterson (1995) reviews and discusses products commercially available as of 5 years ago; and Verity (1997) reviews some current applications, mostly in the telecommunications industry.

Gunter (1996) provides a very readable discussion of the value and dangers of data mining. He points out that the claims for these techniques have been "grandiose." While they can be useful tools, they should not be considered a substitute for more purposive research: using the stored data to test pre-established hypotheses.[17] A somewhat similar message was delivered earlier by Greene and Hield (1992). Dealing with mining of databases in scientific/technical areas, they emphasize that "domain knowledge" is needed to interpret the significance of patterns identified by such activities.

Although the term "data mining" is frequently considered to be an operation performed on numeric data, there is also literature that addresses an area referred to as "text mining." Dwinnell (1999) discusses the challenge of finding patterns in unstructured data, and describes a commercial tool, dtSearch, and some applications of this software, such as resume management. However, it is difficult to determine from his discussion how this software differs from more traditional text management software. More sophisticated research applications are reported on by Smith et al. (1998) and Walker and Truman (1997); they discuss the applications of fuzzy retrieval and neural network technology, respectively, to search and retrieve from large textual archives.

Proper and Bruza (1999) distinguish between information retrieval and information discovery. They state that, while information retrieval has been based on finding documents in fixed collections where users are at least presumed to have a clear understanding of their information need, information discovery is performed on an "open networked environment" where, as a consequence, the document collection is not fixed and where, furthermore, the collection is much more heterogeneous and aggregated. They provide a logical framework for investigating information discovery systems. Fragoudis and Likothanassis (1999) provide an account of using information discovery techniques to find relevant Web links; their approach is based on an autonomous agent that browses the Web.

Although all of these authors are using new terminology, there appears to be much more in common between "text mining" and "information (or knowledge) discovery," on the one hand, and "information retrieval," on the other, than these authors imply. Indeed, many of the techniques for mining text and finding useful links have already appeared in earlier sections of this book dealing with information retrieval, text processing, and intelligent agents.

A useful review of the exploitation of *bibliographic* databases in knowledge discovery applications can be found in a compilation edited by Qin and Norton (1999).

Endnotes

1. This term is used here to refer to any processing of text by computer to perform tasks that involve intelligence when performed by humans. This is not necessarily a widely accepted definition. For example, Sparck Jones (1997) refers to "text processing" only in cases where the complete text is processed as a whole.

2.   Although, as stated in our earlier definition, "intelligent" can also be attributed to the process if it performs a task that humans would need intelligence to accomplish.

3.   For some text processing applications it is necessary for the computer to be able to distinguish among logical components of a document (e.g., title, abstract, main text, footnotes, tables, figures) and to determine relationships among them (such as reading order). This has been referred to, somewhat grandiosely, as "document understanding" (see, for example, Semeraro et al., 1994, and *Proceedings of the Third International Conference on Document Analysis and Recognition*, 1995).

4.   A practical linkage application, involving correspondence and other office documents, is discussed by Pozzi and Celentano (1993).

5.   It is worth noting that modern researchers in text processing use the same measures—recall and precision—first described in the information retrieval literature in the 1950s.

6.   A tool of this type "learns" from a training corpus of text. For example, given a representative set of text extracts known to deal with topic x, it will build a dictionary capable of selecting topic x sentences from a new corpus of text.

7.   In more conventional retrieval exercises, modern text searching methods do not even reach the 50-50 level of performance when much larger databases (hundreds of thousands of items) are involved (Harman, 1993a, b; Sparck Jones, 1995).

8.   The Carnegie Group claimed that its software can categorize a story 10 times faster than a human can.

9.   See Walter (1997) and Katz (1996) for some viewpoints on the ethics of blocking agents of this kind.

10.   A distinction has been made between "server-centric" and "network-centric" searching. In the former, users must first go to a particular information server before applying search strategy. In the latter, the strategy can be applied across many servers (Bock, 1996).

11.   Etzioni (1996), however, has argued that the Web is too "dynamic and chaotic" to be useful in this application.

12.   A completely unrelated problem associated with the Internet is that it is as powerful a tool for disseminating disinformation as it is for making information available (Floridi, 1996).

13.   WordNet is an online lexical database that serves as a kind of electronic thesaurus. Words are organized into sets of synonyms and the synonym sets are linked according to semantic relations (Miller, 1995; Fellbaum, 1998).

14.   See Woodward (1996) for a comprehensive review of the literature dealing with cataloging and classification of Internet resources.

15.   In the business world, the term "data warehouse," rather than "database," seems preferred in this context.

16.   The diversity of potential applications is exemplified by one product, IBM Advanced Scout, "which analyzes NBA basketball game statistics and finds patterns of play coaches can use right away" (Brachman et al., 1996).

17.   The terms "verification-driven" and "discovery-driven" are sometimes used to distinguish hypothesis-testing data mining from the more serendipitous type.

CHAPTER 3

Applications From Other Fields

Artificial intelligence technologies in general, and expert systems in particular, have been applied in virtually all fields of endeavor, including:

Manufacturing
    Cost estimation
    Product design
    Process control

Scheduling/control
    Scheduling of flights and flight crews
    Scheduling in trucking
    Maintenance scheduling (e.g., of aircraft)
    Appointment processing (e.g., in dental offices)
    Course scheduling in schools and colleges

Financial
    Credit checking
    Auditing (see Jacob and Bailey, 1991, for a survey)
    Risk analysis
    Fraud detection
    Market analysis
    Customer services (e.g., "help desks")

Legal (see Bainbridge, 1993, for a survey, and France, 1994, for use of expert systems in drawing up contracts)

Education
    College admissions review
    Course scheduling
    Intelligent tutoring

Environment
    Chemical analysis
    Hazard assessment

Estimation
  Of time to complete a project
  Of costs of production or project completion
Fault analysis (e.g., location of faults or crashes in complex networks or in engineering systems)
Geology
  Mapping
  Rock and fossil identification
  Seismology
Healthcare
  Diagnosis
  Interpretation of medical imagery
  Medical claims processing
  Risk analysis
Social services
  Determining eligibility for public aid
  Providing legal advice to social workers (Hartley et al., 1991)
Human resources management (see Inoue, 1993, for a survey, and Byun and Suh, 1994, for applicability in various human resource situations)
  Recruiting
  Personnel reviews
  Employment counseling (Rapaport, 1996)
Report and correspondence generation
Travel counseling (Sussmann and Ng, 1995)
Political analysis (Duffy and Tucker, 1995)

This is just a very small selection from the many applications described in the literature. Many more can be found in published accounts and, undoubtedly, others exist but have not been reported for reasons of security or competitive advantage. As Bramer (1993) has pointed out: "Today there are thousands, possibly tens of thousands of expert systems in use worldwide. They cover a very wide range of application areas, from archaeology, through munitions disposal to welfare benefits advice" (Page 1).[1] There even exist expert systems to aid in the design of expert systems (Bramer and Milne, 1993).

Artificial intelligence/expert system approaches have also been applied in the humanities but to a lesser extent. Perhaps not surprisingly, humanists tend to be more skeptical about their value. Expert systems may have less obvious practical value in a field such as archaeology but the discipline of building them does force more rigorous analysis of the underlying principles of the field (Ennals and Gardin, 1990).

A special type of expert system application is that associated with response to emergency situations. A system of this kind, designed for emergency response to chemical spills, is described by Zhu and Stillman (1995). Applications of this type seem very appropriate for the expert systems approach because of the great variety of information that may be needed (chemical, biological, physical, geological, and so on) and because of the different backgrounds and levels of training of the personnel involved in the response.

While many of these applications have no obvious relevance to libraries or information centers, others do. Moreover, some otherwise irrelevant applications contain elements that are of potential interest to the library profession.

This section of the book highlights four applications: help desks, medical diagnosis, critiquing systems, and groupware. Help desks are discussed because they perform a type of commercial "reference service" and are dependent on approaches to information retrieval. Diagnosis is included because the diagnostic role of the physician bears some resemblance to the role of the librarian in "diagnosing" information needs. Critiquing systems and groupware are both applicable to library situations, the former to education and training and the latter to various forms of collaboration.

Help desks

A help desk is a telephone service designed to deal with customer questions and problems. Initially, the term referred to a service within the computer industry, established to handle problems encountered within computer networks. While help desks are still strongly associated with the computer industry, services of this kind now exist in a wide range of companies producing consumer products.

The heart of a typical help desk is a "problem-resolution component" in which information is stored on problems previously encountered and possible resolutions to them. The help desk can be considered a true expert system: The support staff who receive the calls are not experts, at least not on all aspects of the situation, but the system gives them problem-solving knowledge. Help desks economize on the number of staff needed to deal with customer questions and reduce the level of the staff assigned to the service. They are made particularly valuable by the fact that many of the problems occur time and time again.

One good example of a help desk is in place at Compaq Computer Corp., as described by Acorn and Walden (1992), which employs a version of the SMART retrieval system developed by Gerard Salton (1997). Use of the system is illustrated in Figures 4 through 7. The cases dealt with in the past (i.e., problems and resolutions) are stored as text descriptions, although described in a brief and formalized way. The staff member receiving a call from a customer enters a text statement of the current problem (Figure 4). The system then looks for similar cases by text search and produces (1) a list of the best-matching cases and (2) questions to ask the customer in order to focus the search and thus retrieve the correct case and resolution. Answers to the questions narrow the scope of the search, although the searcher can browse information on the stored cases (see Figure 5) to supplement the questions. As a result of this interactive process, the cases in the database are given numerical scores that allow them to be ranked according to probable relevance. A score of 70 or above indicates a case that is highly likely to be relevant.

Figure 6 shows an example of a query, with system-generated questions answered by the customer, and the results presented as ranked cases. Figure 7 shows the final record of the process: the problem, the questions, the case retrieved, and the action recommended to the customer. Unresolved cases are analyzed later by specialists and lead to new additions to the database.

Help desks are usually based upon interaction that involves the customer, the customer representative, and the database. The questions generated by the system focus the search more precisely. The answer to a broad question (Is this a frost-free refrigerator?) may frequently restrict further activity to a particular segment of the database (Danilewitz and Freiheit, 1992; Hart and Graham, 1997).

Help desks of the type referred to above operate through case-based reasoning. While there is nothing particularly new in a ranking capability, these systems are unique in that they focus on the most likely solution by generating questions to the user drawn from the cases themselves (e.g., Is this a newly installed printer? Have you tried changing the X? Have you tried cleaning the Y?). The cases in this type of database may be constructed by "case-base authors" and software tools are commercially available to aid in this task. For example, CBR Express (from Inference Corp.) offers a fill-in-the-form interface for this purpose (http://www.inference.com). Allen (1994) reviews business applications of case-based reasoning and compares this approach with rule- or model-based systems, while Chang et al. (1996) discuss the implementation of help desk systems through the use of case-based reasoning; they also mention current limitations of this approach. Law et al. (1997) describe a help-desk system, called Intelligent Help Desk Facilitator (IHDF), which performs fault management in the computer network of a local bank.

Some help desks incorporate sophisticated approaches to natural language processing. For example, Anick (1993) describes such a system, which also includes a form of thesaurus to help users identify alternative search terms. Uthurusamy et al. (1993) describe a diagnostic system that includes highly developed procedures for making

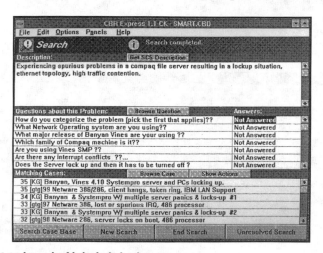

Figure 4   Initial search of help desk database

From T. L. Acorn and S. H. Walden. In: Scott and Klahr, eds. *Innovative Applications of Artificial Intelligence 4*, pp. 3-18. Cambridge, MA, MIT Press, 1992.

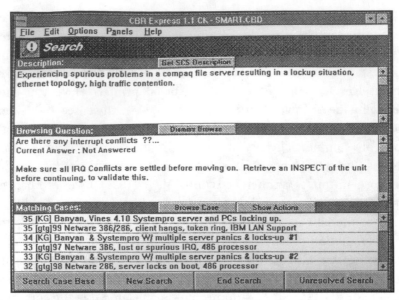

Figure 5   Browsing help desk database for further information

From T. L. Acorn and S. H. Walden. In: Scott and Klahr, eds. *Innovative Applications of Artificial Intelligence 4*, pp. 3-18. Cambridge, MA, MIT Press, 1992.

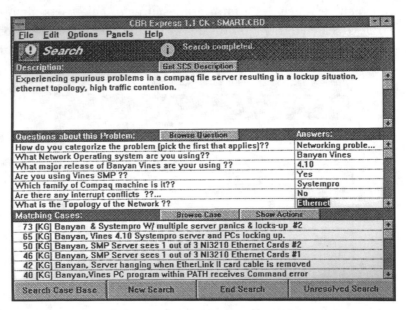

Figure 6   Most highly ranked cases selected on the basis of critical query and customer answers to questions

From T. L. Acorn and S. H. Walden. In: Scott and Klahr, eds. *Innovative Applications of Artificial Intelligence 4*, pp. 3-18. Cambridge, MA, MIT Press, 1992.

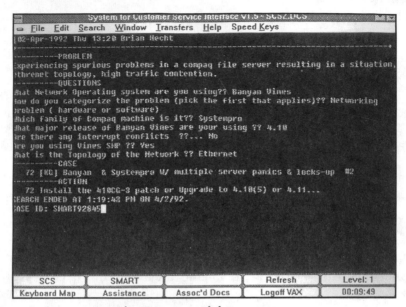

Figure 7   Case summary with action recommended to customer

From T. L. Acorn and S. H. Walden. In: Scott and Klahr, eds. *Innovative Applications of Artificial Intelligence 4*, pp. 3-18. Cambridge, MA, MIT Press, 1992.

ambiguous or poorly formed descriptions (motor vehicle repair records) more intelligible by correcting spelling errors, disambiguating abbreviations, and refining grammar.

Commercially available software for the implementation of help desks, such as Expert Advisor (a product of Software Artistry), may incorporate hypermedia capabilities, with text, graphics, audio, and video files accessible to aid in the diagnostic process as needed. The integration of hypermedia and expert system technologies is reviewed by Ragusa and Turban (1994). Thé (1996) gives a useful survey of commercially available software as of early 1996.

Increasingly, companies heavily involved in customer support activities are seeking to develop help desks that customers can use for themselves, especially help desks that can be implemented through the World Wide Web. Web applications include those discussed by Thurman et al. (1997) for NASA data users and by Foo et al. (2000) for electronics engineers. Software is now commercially available to aid implementation of Web-based help desks (Varney, 1996; Rapoza, 1996b), including software that allows consumers to report problems to a help desk from browsers on their workstations (Walsh, 1996). Because help desks of this type avoid at least some of the help calls that would previously have needed expensive human intervention, the supporting software is sometimes referred to as call-avoidance software (Andrews, 1996).

Other commercially available software is designed to aid the work of help desks—e.g., by storing and retrieving various types of information about customers and their hardware (Seachrist, 1996).

Medical diagnosis

The healthcare community provides many examples of the use of expert systems or systems for which some level of intelligence is claimed. Applications include medical image interpretation (see Piraino et al., 1989; Haug and Beesley, 1992), production of clinical guidelines (e.g., Davis et al., 1995), the direct reporting of clinical evidence (Balas et al., 1996), trend analysis (see Ferri et al., 1992, for application to epidemiologic data), various forms of prediction (as examples see Van Dyne et al., 1994, Laribi and Laribi, 1994, Xu, 1994, and Moynihan et al., 1995, who deal respectively with expert systems for predicting preterm delivery, adverse drug reactions, AIDS susceptibility, and ergonomic ailments), and patient monitoring.

It is in the area of diagnosis, however, that expert systems have had the greatest appeal. The monograph by Berner (1999) surveys clinical decision support systems and includes discussion on selected systems, as well as their mathematical foundations, legal or ethical aspects, and future directions. Research and development in systems for clinical diagnosis has been carried out for many years, and the most recent reports show integration of newer thinking and technologies into system design (Daniel et al., 1997; Reategui, et al., 1997; Hsu and Ho, 1998).

Computer-aided diagnosis has been considered to be a "natural" for an expert systems approach. However, while the artificial intelligence community claims great success with diagnostic systems (see, for example, Weld et al., 1995), the facts indicate otherwise: Diagnostic systems do not perform anywhere close to an expert level and have not been widely adopted by the medical community. Those responsible for developing systems (see Bassoe, 1995, as an example) always seem to claim better results than the physicians who evaluate the systems.

In his review of 30 years of work in this area, Engle (1992) concludes that rather little has been achieved and that the problems involved in producing real-world systems are much greater than was once thought:

> For more than 30 years our group of physicians, statisticians, and computer scientists has worked toward developing a computer program with the capability of a trained physician to make diagnostic decisions in the relatively broad medical subspecialty of hematology. We devised and tested many programs, none of which have been sufficiently useful to warrant carrying beyond the pilot-study stage. We analyzed the reasons for this failure. Our experience confirms the great difficulty, and even the impossibility, of incorporating the complexity of human thought into a system that can be handled by a computer. We concluded that we should stop trying to make a computer act like a diagnostician and concentrate instead on ways of making computer-generated relevant information available to physicians as they make decisions (Pages 216-217).[2]

> In our estimation, the critical impediment to the development of decision programs useful in medicine lies in the impossibility of developing an adequate database and an effective set of decision rules. Any decision module contains only a small fraction of the data and of the intricate relationships that a physician learns in the course of education and practical experience (Page 216).

> Although, over the years, there have been frequent press announcements of medical diagnosis by computer, there are still no generally accepted, successful systems in use except in an experimental way (Page 208).

> Thus, we do not see much promise in the development of computer programs to simulate the decision making of a physician. Well-trained and experienced

physicians develop the uniquely human capability of recognizing common patterns from observation of exceedingly large numbers of stimuli. While people perform this intellectual synthesis quite readily, they are unable to spell out in detail how they do it; hence they cannot transfer the ability to a computer. Neither can they develop this ability, except in a very elementary way, by learning from computer-based programs intended to teach decision making. (Page 216)

Berner et al. (1994) undertook a rigorous evaluation of four commercially available diagnostic systems covering the field of internal medicine in general. The systems were evaluated on their performance in dealing with 105 "diagnostically challenging clinical case summaries involving actual patients." The ranked lists of system-produced diagnoses (cutoff at 20 diagnoses per system) were compared with a ranked list of possible diagnoses prepared by 10 expert clinicians. The proportion of the correct diagnoses (as determined by the experts) contained in the knowledge bases of the four systems ranged from 0.73 to 0.91. The systems ranged from 0.52 to 0.71 success in terms of whether their ranked lists contained the correct diagnosis, but the correct diagnosis rarely appeared at the top of the ranking (the mean rank varied between 5.4 and 12). The investigators conclude that such systems are only usable by physicians who are knowledgeable enough to distinguish between the "good" and the "bad" diagnoses suggested, and they issue the following warning: "Our study arouses concern that important diagnostic considerations may be so obscured by other diagnoses that the value of the program may be significantly decreased, or that it could lead to excessive or costly interventions in inexperienced hands" (Page 1796).

To be sure, diagnostic systems in highly specialized areas of medicine will get better results (see Chang et al., 1994, as one example). However, the claims made for them must always be examined rather closely. For example, Syiam (1994) claims 87 percent success for a system designed to diagnose eye diseases. This seems impressive until one realizes that he included only seven eye diseases in his system.

In his review of the achievements of expert systems in medicine, Salamon (1989) concludes: "…that expert systems have not yet proven to have great practical value. The main reason for this failure seems to be related to initial underestimating of the difficulty of mastering medical knowledge." He adds, "To date, there is sufficient evidence to assert that the original, stated goal of Expert Systems to support physicians in medical decisions may have been a bit presumptuous" (Page 13).

More recently, Coiera (1996) concluded that: "…both AIM [artificial intelligence in medicine] and informatics at present have a minimal impact on the fields that gave them birth" (Page 364). Nevertheless, he is optimistic about the future—in particular, the potential role of the Internet in support of "evidence-based medicine."

Heathfield (1999) discusses the prior 13 years of development in expert systems in medicine, tracing a rise in the 1970s, a disillusionment in the late 1980s and early 1990s, and a rebirth of interest in the late 1990s. In her opinion, the main obstacles are professional and organizational rather than technical.

Critiquing systems

Expert critiquing systems are not really expert systems, in the conventional sense, although they do incorporate knowledge bases of the expert system type. In fact, an expert system may be convertible into an expert critiquing system. A critiquing system is a program that critiques a human solution to a problem (i.e., it critiques the "expert"). Consider the case of medical diagnosis. A critiquing system in this application would accept a diagnosis made by a physician and, using the data on which the physician's diagnosis was based, indicate agreement or disagreement. The feedback, criticism, and explanation provided by the system is intended to improve the human's performance in the future.

One obvious application is in the area of writing. While a simple spell checker, based on simple dictionary lookup, cannot be regarded as a critiquing system, a program designed to improve grammar or style,[3] especially of the more sophisticated type, certainly can. According to Silverman (1992), who has contributed an excellent survey of this field, commercially available programs can locate around

25 percent of the grammar errors and 80 percent of the stylistic errors in typical office documents.

Critiquing systems are also in use in other fields, including computer-aided design, software engineering, and various medical applications. Shepherd (1998) describes a comparison between a critiquing system and a conventional system to assist in the operations of the San Francisco water supply system.

In practice, the boundaries between an expert critiquing system and an intelligent tutoring system are difficult to draw. For example, Obradovich et al. (1996) describe an expert system for antibody identification in blood samples that can be applied as a tutoring system for students or a critiquing system for practitioners.

Properly developed critiquing systems could have applicability in continuing education for several library applications, perhaps most obviously in various reference service tasks.

Groupware

Rasmus (1995, 1996) describes groupware—software designed to facilitate communication, the sharing of information, and collaborative work over networks—including shared memory, shared screen applications, group editing, and desktop video conferencing. Although he refers to the applicability of AI to group applications, there is no evidence that most groupware products exhibit true intelligence.

Groupware can be applied to a number of different activities, most obviously collaborative research[4] and collaborative authorship. Sharma et al. (1994) refer to four classes of groupware: messaging, conferencing, decision-making, and co-authoring systems. Edmonds et al. (1994) discuss an unusually complex application: collaborative engineering design. A group approach to the production of electronic reference works is discussed by Burger et al. (1994), with special emphasis on the problems of distributed management of structured documents.

Collaborative work within a network, whether synchronous or asynchronous, requires efficient sequencing and coordination. Rasmus (1997) discusses the characteristics of workflow tools designed to facilitate group work and the production of group products.

Nunamaker (1997) presents a review of the fundamental issues and research challenges facing researchers in developing group support systems, noting that future research should focus on ease of use, replacing the role of facilitator for day-to-day use, crisis response, and multilingual use, among other things. Grudin and Palen (1997) studied actual calendar use at various organizations to determine best adoption practices for scheduling software. They concluded that the software must first demonstrate that it is useful to the individual above and beyond its use to the group, and that a bottom-up process of adoption, where early adopters exert influence on peers to use the technology, may be the best approach for diffusion of this technology.

Endnotes

1.   Durkin (1993) estimated that more than 12,000 expert systems had been developed by the time of his survey. However, our experience indicates that the great majority of these never went beyond experiment or prototype stages.

2.   See Johannes (1995) for a description of the use of expert systems by HMO clerks dealing with treatment authorization.

3.   As, for example, Grammatik Mac, a product of Reference Software International.

4.   For a discussion on electronic laboratory notebooks, including groupware applications, see Borman (1994).

CHAPTER 4

General Technologies

The handling of speech (as input and output) and visual images by computer, applications that are generally considered to fall within the field of artificial intelligence, are briefly surveyed in this section.

Speech technology

Voice input to computer systems is becoming increasingly important as personal computers get smaller and smaller, and, thus, tactile devices are more difficult to apply successfully.[1] Dictation systems now exist to produce business letters, newspaper articles, or other specialized reports (e.g., radiology results).

The more constrained the conditions, the better that voice-recognition systems will perform. Constraints include:

1. A task-specific vocabulary (e.g., relating to insurance claims or radiology results)

2. The system is tuned to the voice of particular speakers

3. The use of isolated word input is used (the speaker pauses between each word).

While we are still a long way from widely applicable systems, considerable progress has been made in the past 20 years.

Rudnicky et al. (1994) survey the state of the art in this field. They point out that systems calibrated to the voice of a single speaker, and operating under benign conditions (speaker uses head-mounted, noise-canceling microphones), can operate on vocabularies of up to 40,000 words (Markowitz, 1996, claims 100,000 words).

At the other extreme, under the most adverse conditions (telephone input from multiple voices), vocabularies in the range of 10-20 words (e.g., digit recognition for telephone or account numbers) are the limit and, even with such small vocabularies, the system needs to "learn" from very large numbers (several thousand) speakers. Corpora are being constructed to facilitate the development of automatic voice-interactive telephone services—e.g., Macrophone (Taussig and Bernstein, 1994), which incorporates about 200,000 utterances from about 5,000 speakers.

More recent reviews indicate that research and development in speech processing continue but that progress is still slow. Cawkell (1999) discusses the increases in commercialization in this software, citing products by IBM and Dragon Systems as examples. Alleva et al (1998) report on research going on at Microsoft that is aimed at improving the accuracy rate of continuous speech recognition (as contrasted with isolated speech recognition). Both papers reveal that there is still a trade-off between depth and breadth of processing in speech-recognition technology.

Many specialized applications of speech-recognition technology have been described in the published literature. For example, Cass (1992) discusses the use of one commercial product in the generation of medical reports, in this case in the field of endoscopy:

> The physician works at a computer screen displaying a report text with blanks imbedded in it, as well as a list of words to fit in each of the blanks, and instructions to speak the words into a microphone. The computer analyzes the speaker's utterances and picks the words whose sounds are most similar. The physician's choices are then placed in the blank. The physician also uses voice to edit the report form on the screen . . . (Page 969).

This system can be calibrated to the voice of a particular physician for a vocabulary of around 3,000 words drawn from over 2,000 endoscopic reports. A medical dictation system capable of working with the vocabularies of different specialties is available from Kurzweil.

Several voice-driven interfaces, based on limited vocabularies, already exist for Windows and other applications.

Speech synthesis (i.e., computer-generated voice output) is a less difficult problem than voice input. Kukich (1992) claims that voice-recognition technology is not sufficiently advanced to allow for useful speech-to-text translation in the short term. Voice-synthesis technology, on the other hand, is capable of producing reasonably intelligible speech from clean text. She points out that text keyed by a TDD (Telecommunications Device for the Deaf) user can be synthesized with 78 percent intelligibility with no "cleaning." Cleaned text (e.g., with automatic spelling correction applied) can reach 84 percent intelligibility.

Rudnicky et al. (1994) agree that text-to-voice processing systems can operate at a low error rate, but they are still far from sounding "natural." They suggest that this technology has reached a plateau and that further improvements (in voice quality) will be difficult to achieve.

Commercial applications of interactive voice-response systems (e.g., in banking and brokerage) are referred to by Linthicum (1996), who deals mainly with implementation tools and turnkey systems.

Experimental work on speech interfaces continues in a number of fields, including healthcare, where automated history-taking systems (see, for example, Johnson et al., 1993) and systems to aid physicians in recording findings from patient examinations (see, as another example, Shiffman et al., 1993) are of particular interest.

The indexing of sound databases presents problems that are even more complex than those associated with image databases (see next section of the book) and much less work has been done in this area. Sparck Jones et al. (1996) claim that "dialogue retrieval is currently well beyond the speech processing state of the art," and the retrieval of other types of sounds (e.g., from an archive of sounds of potential use to a musician) cause even greater difficulties. Moreover, speech and other sound data impose greater storage and processing requirements than text data.

Experiments in retrieval from collections of spoken messages (e.g., voice mail), reported by Sparck Jones et al. (1996) and Jones et al. (1997), have produced promising results, although the small corpus they worked with was quite artificial: short, prepared messages on limited topics, with very limited vocabularies and few speakers.

Within these constraints, the investigators were able to achieve retrieval results that were between 75 and 95 percent effective as compared with results achieved when searching the same dialogue transcribed into text form.

Modern methods for synthesizing and archiving sounds electronically can make large numbers of sounds available to the musician, but the retrieval of a particular sound from such an archive presents a significant problem. Feiten and Günzel (1994) describe an approach to indexing and retrieval of sounds through use of neural networks. The retrieval index is created automatically.

The ability to recognize and label (i.e., index) sounds automatically has much in common with the processing needed to recognize images automatically. As Picard and Minka (1995) point out, there exists "sound texture" as well as image texture. Thus, it should be possible to develop techniques to identify certain sounds (a bell ringing, water running, applause) automatically using some form of (sound) pattern matching.

The state of the art in the retrieval of sounds is represented in a paper by Blum et al. (1997). They describe a "sound browser" developed to allow fuzzy searches on audio databases. Capabilities include query by example (i.e., "find sounds similar to. . . ").

Another broad overview, spanning the fields of information retrieval, speech processing, audio analysis, and signal processing, but written for the non-specialist, is an article by Foote (1999). He reviews technologies such as keyword spotting, sub-word indexing, speaker identification, and music discrimination. He also provides an overview of the state of the art in advanced audio interfaces, and of the Informedia Project, a research project underway at Carnegie Mellon University, which combines advanced video and audio analysis and text-based information retrieval techniques in building a multimedia digital library (Witbrock and Hauptmann, 1998).

Research on speech interfaces in retrieval applications goes back for several years (see, for example, Smith et al., 1989). Modern approaches are exemplified by the work of Feder and Hobbs (1995).

Kai et al. (1996) deal with the automatic indexing of broadcasts by topic and genre, but they work from the printed text of the broadcast rather than its audio version.

Hauptmann and Witbrock (1997) describe a system for retrieving television news segments on demand. Their approach is to use speech-recognition technology to create text transcripts of the audio portion of the broadcast. The transcripts are stored in a searchable form. Spoken queries can be used to locate and play back a particular segment. The authors claim that their experimental system "is quite useable with only moderate speech recognition accuracy." Mani et al. (1997) discuss related research on methods for retrieval of the video portion of these news broadcasts.

Patel and Sethi (1996) describe methods they developed to classify motion picture segments through audio processing. At present, the system can only identify broad categories (such as "musical") but the authors suggest that it could be refined to more specifically identify types of scene (action scene, dancing scene, romantic scene, and so on). Later (Patel and Sethi, 1997), they extend their research to speaker identification (e.g., of actors in video clips from movies).

As true with other facets of the technologies covered in this book, the more popular trade journals tend to be wildly optimistic about future possibilities. For example, Flynn's (1993) claim was completely unrealisitic:

> By the end of the decade, speech-reccognition systems will let you speak naturally with a virtually limitless vocabulary (Page 29).

Haas (1996), citing Rudnicky, makes an important point relevant to future prospects in this area:

> There is a distinction between speech recognition and speech understanding: speech recognition requires that a system identify the words in an utterance, while speech understanding requires that a system also handle the problems of NL understanding, such as anaphora, ellipsis, and other discourse phenomena. Speech recognition is useful for structured

tasks such as data entry and issuing simple commands, but a dialogue of any kind requires speech understanding (Page 98).

The understanding of human speech by computer is not a prospect that is on the immediate horizon.

It is important to recognize that, even within the community of researchers in this field, there exists a wide divergence of opinion on what speech recognition technology has achieved and what is likely to come in the near term. Levinson (1995), for example, believes that it will be a long time before systems of real commercial value will emerge:

> The majority opinion holds that technical improvements will soon make large-vocabulary speech recognition commercially viable for specific applications. My prediction . . . is that technical improvements will appear painfully slowly but that in 40 to 50 years speech recognition at human performance levels will be ubiquitous. That is, incremental technical advances will, in the near term, result in a fragile technology of relatively small commercial value in very special markets, whereas major technological advances resulting from a true paradigm shift in the underlying science will enable machines to display human levels of competence in spoken language communication. This, in turn, will result in a vast market of incalculable commercial value (Page 9954).

The most comprehensive review of the speech-recognition field can be found in a monograph by Markowitz (1996). See Martin et al. (1996) for the description of a system that can be used by software developers to implement conversational speech applications; the system includes grammar and discourse management components.

Given the wide diversity of viewpoints on the prognosis for speech-recognition technology, it is important to note that there are now ongoing attempts at empirically evaluating its results. Young and Chase (1998) describe the efforts initiated by the federal government in evaluating speech recognition with its CSR (Continuous Speech Recognition) program begun in 1989, which subsequently evolved into the CSR and LVCSR (Large Vocabulary Conversational Speech Recognition)evaluation programs. Like the TREC initiative, already discussed in the context of text retrieval, these make use of common training and test databases, and therefore allow comparisons to be made among algorithms. The goals of these evaluations include comparison of algorithms and/or systems in controlled tests, assessment of performance on specific tasks, and empirical measurement of progress. Most tests have been on speaker-independent continuous speech, with the maximum size vocabulary being about 65,000 words. Error rates appear to range from about 5 percent to 20 percent depending on other variables.

Computer vision

For our purposes, this technology can be divided into: (1) recognition of printed (or, under certain circumstances, handwritten) characters to allow text processing by computer, including input to such tasks as speech synthesis, and (2) recognition of other objects (e.g., faces). The second (and more complex) application has been used successfully in various inspection tasks in industry as well as in various forms of photo interpretation.

The increasing number of image databases that are emerging prompts our interest in computer vision beyond the character-recognition application. The indexing and searching of image databases through computer vision technologies are of great potential interest. Normal approaches to indexing—representing the images by descriptors or other textual elements—is not really satisfactory and is very labor-intensive. Under certain circumstances, a database could be interrogated by "full image search" (analogous to full-text search)—i.e., the system would look for the image that best matches one input by a searcher.

Kurita and Kato (1993) refer to this as "querying by visual example" or as "similarity retrieval." They describe a number of experimental applications, for example:

1. When a trademark is applied for, it can be scanned by a Patent Office and matched against a database of existing trademarks.[2]

2. To query museum or art museum databases, a user can sketch an image (e.g., of a landscape or part of a landscape) and the system will look for paintings that best resemble it.[3]

DiLoreto et al. (1995) discuss work that is somewhat similar to that of Kurita and Kato although in a completely different environment. Their experimental geographic information system, "based only on the pictorial representation of a query," allows a search that can involve use of geometric attributes, topological relationships, and distances. Zhu et al. (1999) describe another geographic application in which both text analysis and image processing are used to produce a Geospatial Knowledge Representation System (GKRS).

The QBIC (Query by Image Content) system, developed by IBM, is being used experimentally in several applications (Flickner et al., 1995). Holt and Hartwick (1994), who have used it in an art history context, describe the capabilities as follows:

> QBIC provides various forms of image queries. The two most general are as an 'object query,' or as an 'image query.' Object queries retrieve images containing objects which match query specifications, such as 'Find shapes that are red and circular,' whereas image queries match overall image characteristics, for example, 'Find images with mostly red and blue tones.' To do object queries, the objects must be identified in each scene, typically manually by outlining them prior to the queries. The process of outlining objects, and then of computing attributes or features for each object and for each image as a whole is referred to as image classification. There are basic drawing tools such as a rectangle, ellipse, polygon, paint brush and a snake tool, which outline the selected images. A fill tool expedites the masking of high contrast images by automatically outlining pixels of a similar value to one selected (Pages 82-83).

QBIC permits searches involving colors, textures, and shapes as well as the subject represented in a painting. It also allows query by example ("find other pictures like this one"). Holt and Hartwick report that searches on shapes in paintings can present considerable problems.[4]

Techniques for recognizing and matching shapes are still very far from perfect. Moreover, as Picard and Minka (1995) point out, shape analysis does not solve all query-by-example problems: Some sought images (a field, water, crowds of people, fire) have no well-defined shape but must, instead, be matched by "texture." They discuss approaches to identifying "visually similar regions" in a picture, using such characteristics as "directionality, periodicity, randomness, roughness, regularity, coarseness, color distribution, contrast, and complexity." The experimental system they developed seeks to mimic human behavior in the recognition of visually similar scenes. Picard (1996) deals further with vision texture in image retrieval.

Gudivada and Raghavan (1995) identify even more complex retrieval situations associated with certain types of image databases, including the representation and retrieval of three-dimensional images ("retrieval by volume") and "retrieval by motion" (i.e., finding an image that depicts a particular action).

For examples of image retrieval systems in which color searching is a major component see Ogle and Stonebraker (1995) and Smith and Chang (1997b).

Agnew et al. (1997) describe an experimental approach to query-by-example searching of images on the World Wide Web. The system will locate the images, index them (by color, size, and other features), and store the indexes on a server. Smith and Chang (1997a) present another approach to indexing Web images, using both textual and visual features, and Rui et al. (1999) discuss the application of relevance feedback in image-retrieval applications.

Work on the "understanding" of pictures is exemplified in Srihari (1993, 1995) and Nakamura et al. (1993), although their research is ancillary to computer vision since they use accompanying text to facilitate recognition of images (photographs of faces in the case of Srihari, elements in a textbook diagram or engineering drawing in the case of Nakamura et al.). Srihari and Zhang (1999) discuss the interactive use of text processing and image processing to optimize retrieval of multimodal documents.

Hauptmann and Wactlar (1997) and Wactlar et al. (1999) describe ongoing work in the Informedia digital library project at Carnegie Mellon University. They have created a terabyte digital video library and use speech, image, and natural language processing in combination to automatically index and retrieve video segments. In an even more ambitious undertaking, Lienhart et al. (1997) describe their attempts at video abstracting, in which they create sequences of moving images much shorter than the original. They use semantic information from the video, and the text and audio that accompany it, to create the abstract, which is then compiled into an HTML page for access on the Web.

Several useful overviews of image indexing and retrieval (especially content-based approaches—those based on properties of the image itself rather than textual descriptions) have been published. They include Grimson and Mundy (1994), Rasmussen (1997), Heidorn (1999), and Forsyth (1999).

The recognition of handwriting continues to be of research interest (see, for example, Nakagawa et al., 1993) since a pen interface[5] to a computer offers a number of interesting possibilities from the querying of databases to the generation of reports without keyboarding. In limited handwriting recognition tasks, such as the recognition of ZIP-code digits, a 96 percent success rate is claimed (see, for example, Fontaine and Shastri, 1993), but general-purpose systems for recognizing handwritten characters are not on the immediate horizon.

The extent of the problem is illustrated in numerous research projects. Jameel (1994) is typical: 877 characters from 13 different writers were used to train his neural network system. Seven characters (letters) from three different writers were used in testing the system. These character sets had not been used in training. Training involved between 10 and 15 million iterations to raise the identification rate to acceptable levels.

The state of the art in the recognition of handwriting (e.g., in the reading of bank checks) is well illustrated in *Proceedings of the Third International Conference on Document Analysis and Recognition* (1995).

Conventional character recognition has shown considerable progress in the last 20 or so years, and omnifont readers are now sufficiently commonplace that this technology need not be discussed further here.[6] "Intelligent character recognition" systems now deal with more difficult problems such as the handling of poor-quality text, the processing of more complex documents (containing text, graphics, and tables), and the recognition of handwritten characters (Mallen, 1992).

The state of the art in commercial applications of handwriting recognition is exemplified by the Palm Pilot, designed and marketed by Palm Computing (http://palmpilot.3com.com). In this case, an unlimited set of words is "recognized," but the user must write in a stylized fashion.

Endnotes

1. Rudnicky et al. (1994) believe that it is unlikely that speech input devices will replace keyboards completely.

2. The trademark searching situation is also addressed by Wu et al. (1995).

3. Benois-Pineau et al. (1997) describe a similar approach in which images of buildings can be retrieved by matching a "synthesized sketch."

4. For a discussion of shape-recognition techniques and their relative effectiveness see Mehrotra and Gary (1995) and Mehtre et al. (1997). Jagadish (1996) evaluates one approach.

5. Pen interfaces are already in use but tend to be based on the marking of words displayed on an online "palette" by circling, crossing through, underlining, and so on (see, for example, Poon and Fagan, 1994).

6. Neverthless, OCR scanning is still far from perfect. For example, the scanning of a 250 MB database of items from the *Federal Register*, at the 1996 Text Retrieval Conference (TREC-5), produced error rates between 5 percent and 20 percent, depending upon the version used for scanning (Voorhees and Kantor, 1996).

CHAPTER 5

Conclusions and Implications

Before discussing the implications of our survey for libraries and information services, some comments on the field of AI/ES in general seem necessary.

As pointed out early in the book, there exist many interpretations of what the terms "artificial intelligence" and "expert systems" really mean. If a system has to "behave intelligently" (e.g., make inferences or learn from its mistakes) to qualify as one having AI, few such systems exist in any application. On the other hand, if one accepts that a system exhibits AI if it does things that humans need intelligence to do, many more systems would qualify. One example can be drawn from the field of subject indexing. Many programs have been developed to select subject terms for documents, usually by extraction but sometimes by limited assignment. Most such programs operate largely on frequency criteria or by matching words/phrases in text with words/phrases highly associated with a limited set of descriptors or category codes. Such programs, in themselves, exhibit no intelligence. Nevertheless, they can be considered "intelligent" by virtue of the fact that a human would need to use intelligence to perform the same task.

Strict and loose definitions can also apply to the term "expert system." A strict definition can be based on the structure/components of the system or, alternatively, on its performance. The former would insist that the system have all the necessary parts (knowledge base, inference engine, user/system interface), together with some necessary actions (e.g., explaining its own decisions), while the latter would require that the system behave at the level of the expert. A more relaxed definition would consider any system an expert system if it can help the non-expert perform some task at a level closer to that of the expert, whether or not all the essential components are in place. For example, the Hepatitis Knowledge Base, maintained for several years by the National Library of Medicine, could be considered an expert system if it were used by general practitioners to make better diagnoses or select better treatments in this area, even though no inference engine was applied to it. If "behave at the level of an expert" is an essential component of the definition of "expert system," it is improbable that any such systems exist in any field.

In this book, we have assumed rather loose definitions of both terms to avoid needless hairsplitting on what to include and what not.

The history of AI/ES technologies to date can be divided roughly into three phases. The first was characterized by wild optimism regarding the problems that could be solved and the profits that could be made. This phase can be considered to extend through the 1960s, 1970s, and most of the 1980s. The second phase, beginning in the 1980s, was one of disillusionment. The technologies had not lived up to their expectations in terms of the problems they could solve, were not as widely adopted as anticipated (see, for example, Shao et al., 1995, for a discussion of their limited impact on the banking industry), and had not generated the profits expected. By the early 1990s, many of the larger companies had bowed out of the AI/ES field and many of the smaller ones, founded on these technologies, had either disappeared or had merged with other entities. By 1994 (No more expert systems, 1994), the field was virtually written off in some quarters. Raggad (1996) suggests that only around 10 percent of the medium- to large-sized expert systems implemented in industry could be considered a success.[1]

We now seem to be at the beginning of a third phase characterized by a return to the enthusiasm or, perhaps, overenthusiasm of earlier years. The reason, of course, is the explosive growth of the Internet in general and the World Wide Web in particular. The Internet creates new applications, modifies existing ones, and facilitates collaborative projects in the implementation of systems.[2] As Schmuller (1996) points out: "New companies (and new divisions within existing organizations) have sprung up: their goal is to infuse Web sites with intelligent capabilities and thereby help businesses acquire new customers and provide enhanced service. They also develop intelligent agents that streamline your interaction with the Web" (Page 8).

Software is now being produced to assist companies and other organizations to implement network-accessible expert systems for themselves—e.g., for customer product selection (Huntington, 1997).

While the Internet may indeed have changed the situation in terms of the size of the market and the viability of various implementations, it does not change it in terms of basic capabilities.[3] Unfortunately, the published literature continues to include completely wild and unjustifiable claims, as in the following: "AI will someday produce viable intelligent clones, capable of learning from natural language or broad enough in skill and knowledge to make 'educated guesses' when confronted with questions from left field" (Rasmus, 1995, page 27).

Such extreme statements are more likely to appear in popular technical magazines than in the more scholarly literature. The fact remains, however, that the computing community's views of what has been achieved, or is likely to be achieved, almost always differ from the views of the practitioner community—those involved in the actual use of the systems. A typical example of this occurs in the field of medical diagnosis. A report from the American Association for Artificial Intelligence (Weld et al., 1995) claims: "These systems have achieved a high level of effectiveness, size, speed, and accuracy for tasks such as diagnosing diseases and suggesting treatments in human medical care..." (Page 58).

On the other hand, Kassirer (1994), editor of the *New England Journal of Medicine*, who has had many years of experience with such systems and participated in the development of several early prototypes, is less enthusiastic:

> A major limitation to the improvement of these programs is a further expansion of their knowledge bases to include a larger and larger proportion of the diseases encountered by physicians. Most research groups have given up trying to accomplish this task, which is tedious, unrewarding, and endless because the currency of the program's knowledge base must be maintained as diseases become better understood and new diagnostic tests arise (Page 1824).

Some writers do attempt to paint a more realistic picture of the capabilities and potentials of the more advanced technologies. For example, Bainbridge (1993) puts it this way:

> The phrase 'expert system' conjures up images of an intelligent computer system that will outperform and, eventually, replace human experts. Such visions are far from reality and demonstrate a considerable misunderstanding of the nature of expert systems (Page 25).

and, from our own field, Weckert (1991) has said:

> No machine can be made to function in the way that a human does, because of the different stuff of the hardware. For the same reason, in many fields of human expertise, no expert system will be as expert as the human expert. It may be that in the future truly expert systems will be built, but they will need to be constructed using hardware which is very similar . . . in composition, form, and structure, to humans (Page 112).

He goes on to maintain that truly expert systems cannot be developed but *useful* systems certainly can.

Dreyfus and Dreyfus (1986) have probably been the strongest critics of artificial intelligence approaches in general:

> Computers as reasoning machines can't match human intuition and expertise . . . (Page xi).

> Human intelligence can never be replaced with machine intelligence simply because we are not ourselves 'thinking machines' in the sense in which that term is commonly understood (Page 102).

> It is highly unlikely that expert systems will ever be able to deliver expert performance . . . we'd prefer to call them 'competent systems' . . . (Page 102).

> In any domain in which people exhibit holistic understanding, no system based upon heuristics will consistently do as well as experienced experts, even if those experts were the informants who provided the heuristic rules (Page 109).

They base their conclusions, in large part, on the fact that human expertise is very dependent on experience and intuition, and it is these human qualities, rather than codifiable knowledge, that computers can never provide. This point, also emphasized by other writers, e.g., Bainbridge (1991), will be returned to later.

Forslund (1995) takes a somewhat different approach, arguing that it is more realistic to seek "advice-giving" systems capable of helping in a wider range of problems than "expert systems" that seek actual solutions to a smaller range; advice-giving systems are less "brittle."

The information service environment

Exaggerated claims for AI/ES technologies, and overoptimism regarding their potential contributions, are as prevalent in domains of direct relevance to libraries and information services as they are in other fields. In particular, the report from the American Association for Artificial Intelligence (AAAI) (Weld et al., 1995) claims that the AI community can have a significant positive impact on the Internet and, in the U.S., on the National Information Infrastructure (NII).

The AAAI study suggests several AI applications of relevance to the NII and, therefore, to the digital library, including intelligent interfaces, knowledge discovery services, and integration and translation services. These are all highly related and one application merges naturally into another, with all three falling into the "intelligent agent" area reviewed earlier in the book.

These applications are described by Weld et al. (1995) in highly optimistic terms:

> Interfaces will need to be intelligent, adjusting automatically to a person's skills and pattern of usage. An intelligent interface to NII resources could help people find

and do what they want, when they want, in a manner that is natural to them, and without their having to know or specify irrelevant details of NII structure (Page 47).

Integration and translation services might convert information from one format to another subject to semantic constraints. For example, a financial translation service would not just perform the unit conversion from Japanese yen into U.S. dollars, but could convert from raw cost to total cost, including import duties, taxes, and fees (Page 47).

Knowledge discovery services could track the creation of new databases and updates to existing repositories. These services could cross-index related topics to discover new correlations and produce summaries (Page 47).

Users should not be forced to remember the details of particular databases or the wide and growing variety of services and utilities to use them effectively. Instead, the system should support an understandable, consistent interface that tunes itself to the task at hand. . . . Users should be able to form arbitrary questions and requests easily, without being limited by restrictive menus or forced to learn artificial query languages. Intelligent interfaces should accept requests in whichever modality (e.g., speech, text, gestures) the user chooses (Page 49).

Personal assistant agents should adapt to different users, both by receiving direct requests from the user and by learning from experience (Page 49).

Intelligent user interfaces could act as assistants to both novice and expert users, helping them navigate the NII's labyrinth of databases and efficiently interact with advanced services. By responding to high-level requests in spoken language and other natural modalities, by communicating information both verbally and graphically, by automatically determining how and when to accomplish the goals of individual users, and by adapting to the skills and desires of those users, personal assistant agents will allow humans to benefit from information resources and facilities that might otherwise overwhelm them with their size, complexity, and rate of change (Page 49).

Machine-learning algorithms . . . [offer] the promise of programs that examine gigabytes of network-accessible data to extract trends that would otherwise go unnoticed by people (Page 56).

Machine learning techniques could lead to electronic news readers that learn the interests of each user by observing what they read, then use this knowledge to automatically search thousands of news sources to recommend the ten most interesting articles. Similar applications include building intelligent agents that provide current awareness services, alerting users to new Web pages of special interest, or providing "What's New" services for digital libraries (Page 56).

While the more modest of these functions do seem attainable (and, indeed, have already been achieved to some extent by existing agents), others are beyond our present capabilities and, if one can believe such critics as Dreyfus and Dreyfus (1986), will remain so.

Such optimistic descriptions suggest that most of the problems faced by the user, or the librarian, in trying to locate relevant information in vast network resources (or, indeed, most of the problems grappled with by researchers in information retrieval over the last 40 or more years) are close to solution. A superficial browsing of the report might certainly give such an impression. A closer examination, on the other hand, shows that the report is primarily a wish list—a call for significant levels of funding in areas where successes have so far been very limited.

Careful study of the AAAI report shows that even this community recognizes the problems that exist, that successes have so far been modest, and that we are very far from being able to replace the human expert in any application:

> Building ontologies is difficult for three reasons. First, articulating knowledge in sufficient detail that it can be expressed in computationally effective formalisms is hard. Second, the scope of shared background knowledge underlying interactions of two agents can be enormous. For example, two doctors collaborating to reach a diagnosis might combine common-sense conclusions based on a patient's lifestyle with their specialized knowledge. Third, there are unsolved problems in using large bodies of knowledge effectively, including selecting relevant subsets of knowledge, handling incomplete information, and resolving inconsistencies (Page 61).

> Ontology construction is difficult and time consuming and is a major barrier to the building of large-scale intelligent systems and software agents (Page 61).

and, speaking of man-machine natural language communication:

> These abilities, in their most general form, are far beyond our current scientific understanding and computing technology (Page 61).

and, finally, and most tellingly:

> These techniques often prove to be brittle and non-robust under real-world conditions (Page 63).

Here they were referring to an unusually difficult task, computer recognition of visual images but, as we have seen in this survey, very few "real-world" applications, incorporating artificial intelligence and expert system technologies, exist in any field and it is likely to be a very long time before these technologies will make a significant contribution in facilitating the operations of the digital library.

To be really valuable, systems must be large enough, general enough, and robust enough to deal with real-world problems. Unfortunately, systems that work well at experimental or prototype stages, using limited data, rarely scale-up successfully to the handling of more general problems and more realistic volumes of data. This situation has been well addressed by Jacobs (1994), at least for the area of text processing:

> Many of the more ambitious goals of artificial intelligence have proved unattainable because of the failure of the many small, successful systems to 'scale up.' The general use of technologies such as natural language interfaces and expert systems has done little to alleviate the basic difficulties and overwhelming cost of knowledge engineering. At the same time, emerging text processing techniques, including data extraction from text and new text retrieval methods, offer a means of accessing stores of information many times larger than any organized knowledge base or database.

> Although knowledge acquisition from text is at the heart of the information management problem, interpreting text, paradoxically, requires large amounts of knowledge, mainly about the way words are used in context. In other words, before 'intelligent' text processing systems can be trained to mine for useful knowledge, they must already have enough knowledge to interpret what they read. The point at which there is 'enough,' dubbed 'the crossover point' by Doug Lenat, is still a matter of debate, as no real program seems close to having enough knowledge to achieve general human-like understanding (Page 235).

Library applications so far

As discussed earlier in the book, many expert systems have been developed within libraries or schools of library and information science. Almost without exception, these have never moved beyond experimental or prototype stages, and most projects have been completely discontinued. This agrees with the findings of other reviewers (e.g., Poulter et al., 1994). Indeed, in some cases at least, the "system" described existed only in the mind of the author. It is necessary to look at the reasons behind this state of affairs before proceeding to a discussion of future prospects.

Many of these applications in the library field can best be referred to as "solutions in search of a problem." The developers, by and large, seem to have been naively optimistic regarding both system capabilities and system costs. The fact that software designed for expert system implementation was an inexpensive purchase appears to have misled many into the belief that expert systems could be put into operation cheaply. But the software is a trivial component of the total cost. Even for a system of very modest scope, the amount of effort needed for knowledge acquisition, and for reducing this to system form (rule-based, frame-based, case-based, or whatever), can be very great. Moreover, except under very unusual circumstances, the knowledge base thus created will not be static; in many cases it will require regular updating, another time-consuming and costly operation.

A. G. Smith (1996), who has implemented expert systems in library applications in New Zealand, suggests that many library applications were a misuse of expert systems software—the shell was not used to develop a true expert system and few, if any, demonstrated any intelligence.

The truth is that the expert systems developed in the library field are little more than toys compared with operational systems in use in other environments. Systems that address significant problems successfully do not come cheaply. Allen (1994) goes so far as to suggest that these costs make expert systems an unattractive proposition for even commercial enterprises:

"The knowledge-engineering effort associated with traditional expert systems is too costly for the average customer service organization to undertake" (Page 41).

He goes on to explain that this argues for the use of a case-based reasoning approach in such applications (help desks) because companies must usually maintain the necessary records (cases) anyway.

Whether viewed in terms of money or effort, a robust system designed to deal with real-world problems can be very expensive: 8 to 10 person years, or around half a million dollars, just for the development work, is not unusual. A system known as Pharos, developed in the U.K. to advise businesses of European Community legislation that might affect their products, was said to cost more than $1.25 million for development alone.

There is another, related matter that is frequently overlooked. Few librarians have the knowledge or experience needed to implement an expert system or to attempt to apply artificial intelligence techniques to library-related problems. In this they are no different from professionals in other fields. The systems that are successfully operating in other environments have not been developed by their practitioners alone but by the practitioners working closely with companies specialized in the field of knowledge engineering.

Finally, library applications are in many ways more complex than seemingly similar situations elsewhere. For example, an expert system is more likely to be successful as a concierge (Cho et al., 1996) than as a reference librarian because the questions dealt with by the former are more limited and predictable.

Applications of advanced technologies in the library of the future

In considering possible futures, it is necessary to make a distinction between (a) librarians exploiting advanced technologies developed by others, and (b) librarians involving themselves in the design and implementation of systems incorporating these technologies. Both topics will be dealt with.

In looking at prospects, too, it seems sensible to emphasize the role of these technologies in a possible future digital library environment rather than one based primarily on printed resources.

The term "digital library" can have several possible meanings. At one extreme, it can be merely a personal library of information resources maintained by an individual in electronic form. At the other extreme, it can be considered the totality of resources in digital form that can be accessed through networking capabilities. For the purpose of the present discussion, however, a digital library is more like a traditional library, at least conceptually; it is a library maintained by a university, corporation, or other entity to serve a particular community of users.

The objectives of such a digital library are no different from those of a conventional library: to make available to users the information resources they need at the time that they need them and to help users exploit these resources effectively and efficiently. In the digital library, however, most if not all of the resources will be in electronic form, and the great majority will be in a form that is "accessible" rather than "distributed."

Some see the library of the future as not having any "collection" of its own. It would be a mere switching center, referring users to potentially appropriate points in the vast network of resources accessible through the Internet or its successors. Others see the library as primarily a switching center but having important value-adding functions: creating guides, indexes, annotations, and other tools tailored to the needs and interests of the library's own community of users and designed to improve the intellectual accessibility of those network resources likely to have greatest relevance and value to this community.

More farsighted observers (notably Atkinson, 1990, 1993) recognize that the library cannot survive as a mere switching center, even a value-added switching center. To justify its existence in the electronic world, the library must continue to perform one of the most important functions it now performs in the print-on-paper world: to organize the universe of resources in such a way that those most likely to be of value to the user community are made most accessible to this community, physically and intellectually. This implies that the library must act as an information filter, selecting the most relevant resources from the universe of network resources and downloading these to local storage/access facilities. Moreover, the downloaded resources will need to be organized intellectually and themselves made available to users at different levels or tiers of accessibility. Atkinson (1996) makes an important distinction between a "control zone" of network resources extracted and controlled by the library community and an "open zone" of everything else.

One library that has already gone a long way toward the adoption of collection development policies for electronic resources is the Mann Library at Cornell University, as discussed by Demas et al. (1995). They identify various levels or "tiers" of access, illustrated in Figure 8 (see next page). Note that some high-demand items may be downloaded from the national network to the campus network while others are merely accessible from the national network on demand (possibly through the aid of "pointers" provided locally).

Based largely on this model provided by the Mann Library, one can now visualize the digital library as one providing various levels of access to electronic resources, as illustrated in Figure 9 (see page 121). Electronic resources in great demand (level A) are made permanently accessible through a campus or company network, while others (level B) can be accessed remotely via the network when needed (e.g., through the Internet). These are strongly linked to the library because the library may have been responsible for selecting the level A resources from the international network and downloading them to the institutional network. It may also have been responsible for building the indexes or providing the pointers that draw attention to the level B resources.

Alternatively, the level B resources may be brought personally to the attention of individual users by reference librarians consulted face-to-face, by telephone or through electronic mail. The level C and D resources are not available through the campus network but must be used within the library through a local area network or a single dedicated workstation.

Almost twenty years ago, in writing about the future of abstracting and indexing services, Lancaster and Neway (1982) visualized an online filtering system that would eventually bring relevant journal information to individual users. The conceptualization is shown in Figure 10 (see page 122). It assumed that, given that journals exist in electronic form and include abstracts, acceptable "accessing databases" could be built directly from the primary literature. A series of filters (really subject profiles) would be necessary to form major discipline-oriented and mission-oriented databases from all items newly added to all databases (i.e., not restricted to a particular set of journals). More refined filters would form more specialized databases from the first-level databases. User interest profiles could then be applied to the second-level databases. An individual user, then, could log on to some system and be informed that X items, matching his or her profile of interest, have been published since the system was last used. The user may then view abstracts and, if required, get online access to the complete item. Rather than "subscribing" to any one electronic journal, the filters would keep users informed of everything matching their interests wherever published. At various levels, databases

---

Tier 1

> Delivered over the campus network via the Mann Library Gateway. Anticipated high demand and need for quick response and manipulation time dictate the use of media and software that will provide very fast response time.

Tier 2

> Delivered over the campus network via the Mann Library Gateway. Must be interactively available, but a relatively low number of simultaneous uses is expected and slower retrieval time acceptable. Therefore a slower storage medium, such as optical platter, may be acceptable.

Tier 3

> Resources that can be delivered online via the Gateway on demand, but are not continuously available online. Tier 3 resources may be mounted on request for Gateway access or may be used in the library at any time.

Tier 4

> Resources that are available in the library only (i.e., not delivered over the campus network), but that are available from many public access workstations within the library over a local area network.

Tier 5

> Resources that are available in the library only, at single user stations.

Figure 8   Levels of access to electronic resources identified at the Mann Library, Cornell University
From Demas et al. (1995) by permission of the American Library Association.

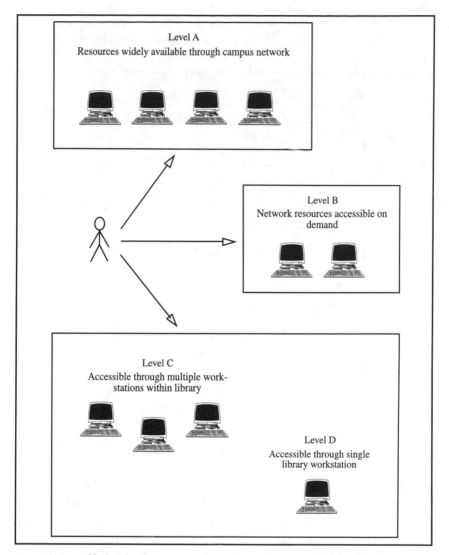

Figure 9 Possible levels of access to electronic resources provided by the library in an academic setting

of abstracts would be available for searching when specific information needs arise.

The model of Figure 10 is highly appropriate to the present information environment made possible by the Internet, although it is probably the library community that should be most heavily involved in building the necessary filters, especially those that are closest to the individual user.

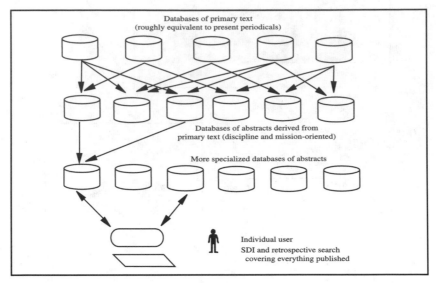

Figure 10   Filtering levels in a digital library environment

Moreover, libraries will be concerned with filtering all types of resources and not just those that are the equivalents of the present journal articles.

In a highly developed digital information network, one can visualize a situation in which an individual builds a personal database by down-loading from network resources the text and graphics of most direct interest. This individual may be supported by some form of institutional library (maintained perhaps by a university, college, or company) which has also downloaded from the broader network the text and graphics most likely to be of value to the institutional community. The situation is depicted in simple form in Figure 11. If an important role of the institu-tional library is to "feed" the personal databases of its users in a dynamic way (e.g., through some form of profile matching), the most obvious evaluation criterion would relate to the frequency with which an indi-vidual needs to go beyond personal and institutional resources to satisfy a particular need. Presumably, if the institutional library was doing an excellent job, most of the individual's needs would be satisfied from his/her own database, some from the institutional database, and very little from the wider network resources.

It is clear that the vast expanse of poorly organized resources that are accessible, at least in a theoretical sense, through the Internet make the construction of effective filters a daunting proposition, whether at individual or institutional levels. Moreover, we are assured that the situation will get much worse. The report from the American Association for Artificial Intelligence (Weld et al., 1995), dealing with the National Information Infrastructure, puts it this way: "Current trends in semiconductor density, processor speed, and network bandwidth suggest that the infrastructure will be thousands of times larger than existing

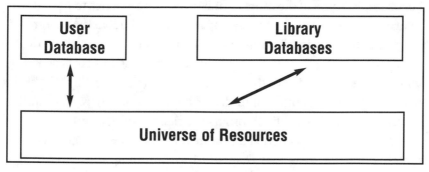

Figure 11   Interacting components in a digital library network

systems such as the Internet; the array of services supported by the NII will be unimaginably vast" (Page 45).

Implications for managers of libraries and other information services

Whether or not one accepts them as truly "expert" or as truly "intelligent," it is quite obvious that information processing tools of ever-increasing sophistication will continue to be developed, and many will become commercially available. Some of these will be of direct relevance to librarians and other providers of information services. They will presumably include improved browsers and search engines for the exploitation of network resources, filtering agents to assist in the management of e-mail and in the selective dissemination of information, powerful data mining programs, resource (i.e., database) selection tools, retrieval software applicable to the searching of databases internal to industrial and other organizations (especially better methods for the searching of large bodies of full text and of various types of images), and more user-friendly interfaces in general (including, perhaps, some limited-application speech-based and pen-based interfaces).

Many of these relevant developments may occur in environments that are quite distant from the field that we think of as "library and information science," and they will be described in other literatures. For example, some of the more sophisticated approaches to interactive information retrieval, incorporating relevance feedback and ranked output, have been implemented in the customer support (help desk) application, while the more successful approaches to text processing tend to be associated with the news industry in general. Clearly, this is because these are multimillion dollar applications where substantial investments can be justified from a cost-benefit standpoint.

It should also be recognized that developments will occur in completely different areas that may still have some applicability in the operation of information services or in education and training activities. For example, expert critiquing systems seem well suited for use in training and re-training for "reference work," and other computer-based approaches may be adapted for instructing library users in information-seeking skills.

In a technological environment that is constantly changing, and especially one in which library services can be expected to become increasingly "digital," it is extremely important for librarians to keep themselves well informed concerning new products and new developments of the type referred to in this book. This is needed not only for the betterment of library services but also because the librarian may be in a good position to bring relevant new technologies to the attention of other parts of the organization (e.g., those responsible for the handling of a company's correspondence files, contract files, engineering drawings, image databases, and so on) and to participate in the evaluation of these technologies. Indeed, some writers (e.g., Raitt, 1993) suggest that the assessment of new information technologies (in the broadest sense and not just those directly related to library services) should be a major function of the librarian of the future. In Appendix 4 we have compiled a list of sources that can be used to monitor new technological products and developments.

To what extent should librarians continue to involve themselves in the design and implementation of their own "intelligent" or "expert" systems? This question is much more difficult to answer definitively.

Of course, "knowledge engineering" is an occupation that may sound glamorous to many librarians and, indeed, some have urged that librarians get involved in the design of more sophisticated systems rather than being merely the users of systems developed by others (see, for example, von Wahlde and Schiller (1993); Drabenstott (1994); LaGuardia (1995); and Brin and Cochran (1994)).

Nevertheless, the fact that pitifully few systems developed within the library field itself have moved beyond experimental or demonstration stages does not encourage one to recommend that the directors of libraries should commit many resources to further work of this type. As pointed out already, the development and maintenance of systems robust enough to handle significant information processing problems is a very expensive proposition, and purchase of the necessary software is a trivial component of the total cost.[4] Furthermore, the great majority of librarians lack the necessary expertise in this area. Knowledge engineering has emerged as a separate discipline, and the companies that operate successfully in this field have achieved considerable experience in system development; their professionals are drawn from fields—e.g., computer science, psychology, linguistics—beyond our own. The knowledge engineering component of other professions is a specialization in its own right. The most obvious example is medicine. The typical practitioner in medicine is not a specialist in medical informatics and is not well qualified to develop sophisticated systems to support various aspects of healthcare. By the same token, most librarians would be well advised not to dabble in a field in which, in all probability, they lack the necessary experience and expertise. Nevertheless, like medical practitioners, they obviously must work closely with the knowledge engineers in any system development of direct relevance to library service.

There are other factors that need to be taken into account. The library-related activities that could most readily be taken over by computers tend not to be complex enough or critical enough—one could not justify the significant expenditures that would be needed to develop systems that would replace humans in performing the task, at least at the single-library level. On the other hand, the most complex and most professional of tasks—those associated with the role of information consultant in the widest sense of the term—are not easily delegated to machines and are not likely to benefit substantially from technology in the foreseeable future.

Sparck Jones (1991) is one writer who has stated the case most clearly. Discussing the information retrieval situation, she maintains that we should not overestimate the potential contribution of artificial intelligence. On the one hand, the sophisticated search, retrieval, and evaluation activities associated with the work of skilled information intermediaries, especially those involved in information analysis functions, are well beyond the capabilities of present computing. On the other hand, the relatively shallow approaches employed by library users in typical catalog or database searches are an inappropriate or unnecessary application of artificial intelligence.

Nevertheless, while one cannot encourage individual libraries to invest resources in standalone systems, there may be applications of sufficient importance to justify investment by the library community at large. That is, larger bodies—consortia or professional associations—may seek funding to address problems of collective interest. In such enterprises, it will be necessary for designated professional librarians to work closely with companies that are fully experienced in knowledge engineering activities.

It seems obvious that any such investment should look to emerging and future needs—problems and services associated with the digital library environment rather than that of print on paper. This suggests that the areas worth pursuing would be those related to the efficient exploitation of network resources on behalf of library users—e.g., improved tools for the implementation of current awareness services, for the evaluation of network resources, for the "feeding" of personal electronic databases, for the creation of new composite documents from dispersed network resources, and so on. Atkinson's (1996) important distinction between a "control zone" of resources controlled by the library community (in much the same way that they now control distributed artifacts through cataloging, classification, indexing and related activities) and an "open zone" of everything else is significant here. Artificial intelligence/expert system technologies may be applicable to some of the "control zone" activities of libraries. Appendix 5 contains some guidance, taken from other authors, on applications for which an expert system approach may be appropriate.

Of course, the commercial world is already producing search engines, intelligent agents, and other tools for the exploitation of networked resources. However, commercial interests, dominated by profit-making motives, do not always coincide with the interests of libraries and their users. Moreover, some library concerns, such as the consistent cataloging of network resources, may not have much commercial appeal.[5]

Basden (1994) suggests that there are three possible levels of benefits associated with expert systems: feature benefits, task benefits, and role benefits. "Feature benefits" refers to an improved way of using some feature or facility, such as a better interface for searching online catalogs or databases. "Task benefits" refers to an improved way of understanding some task, as in machine-aided approaches to indexing. "Role benefits," on the other hand, refers to the ability to use sophisticated technology to perform roles not undertaken before or not possible before. So far, the library community seems to have focused on the feature or task benefits. Probably it would be better if future collective effort went into the possibility of using artificial intelligence/expert system technologies to achieve role benefits, perhaps to deal more deeply with knowledge discovery problems (as exemplified by Swanson's, 1993, work on disconnected literatures) or to exploit databases in forms of technological or social forecasting (Lancaster and Loescher, 1994).

In concluding this book, it is necessary to point out that expert systems are not without their dangers. Weckert and Ferguson (1993) raise some ethical concerns: Reference librarians can make moral judgments (e.g., not to provide information on how to make a bomb or how to commit suicide), but inanimate systems cannot. It has also been pointed out that a significant barrier to the further development of diagnostic systems in the medical field is the possibility of misdiagnosis with attendant litigious consequences (Warner, 1988; Bainbridge, 1991; Allaërt and Dusserre, 1993). Of course, malpractice suits are less likely in the library environment than in healthcare, and the ethical concerns are probably most applicable in only the public library situation. Nevertheless, one must be aware that such concerns do exist. Intelligent network agents may also present various technological dangers. Ordille (1996) points out that agents operating within the Internet can damage servers and that, conversely, servers can damage agents.

There is, however, a more serious issue. A large component of "expertise" is informal and experiential in character (Bainbridge, 1991); the recorded knowledge, however detailed and comprehensive, still requires evaluation and interpretation. People do not become experts merely by having an expert knowledge base available to them. Indeed, the very availability of such a tool can be dangerous, for it puts decisions and actions that are properly the domain of the expert into the hands of the less qualified. To give a concrete example, an expert system applied to "reference work" is no substitute for the experience and intuition of a skilled reference librarian. The system may help a library user, or an inexperienced librarian, to perform competently but not expertly. Over the longer term, too much reliance on technology could have very undesirable consequences— e.g., the truly expert reference librarian might disappear. This danger was well recognized by Dreyfus and Dreyfus (1986): "To the extent that junior employees using expert systems come to see expertise as a function of large knowledge databases and masses of inferential rules, they will fail to progress beyond the competent level of their machines" (Page 121).

These various concerns, together with the fact that rigorous evaluations applied to decision-making systems (from those applied in library reference work to those applied to clinical diagnoses) have produced uninspiring results, strongly suggest that the library community should not be overly optimistic concerning the immediate potential value of these technologies.

Technologically advanced systems may have a useful role to play in the emerging digital library environment, but it is important to recognize their limitations and the fact that they do not reduce our need to continue to develop our human expert resources. Horton (1982) was correct in pointing out that skilled human resources, rather than "machines," are the real capital asset of the Information Age. Harris (1992) has warned that the library profession may be losing control over its "knowledge base" and abandoning its "service ideal," leading to "deprofessionalization" and the eventual demise of the profession. We must not let overreliance on technology, or overoptimism regarding its capabilities, lead us to settle for competence or mediocrity in place of true excellence.

Endnotes

1. Of course, not all writers paint such a negative picture. For example, Hayes-Roth and Jacobstein (1994) imply that any failures that occurred were due mostly to factors beyond the technology itself, such as unreasonable expectations of what could be done and the problems involved in integrating the technology into existing organizational structures. Nevertheless, they acknowledge that there were only a "few parts of it [i.e., the technology] that were mature enough or reliable enough for predictable commercial application." See Killingsworth and McLeod (1992) for a discussion of factors affecting the acceptance and feasibility of expert systems.

2. Nevertheless, while the World Wide Web has greatly increased interest in some applications of the technologies covered in this book, such as intelligent agents, it has perhaps reduced the relevance of some forms. There are a number of cases in which expert system shells have been abandoned in favor of hypertext approaches. Or, rule-based/frame-based approaches have given way to case-based expert systems.

3. Another phenomenon must be noted: the Internet and the World Wide Web are bringing new research groups to the field of information retrieval with the result that techniques described in the literature many years ago are being rediscovered. To mention but one example, Fowler et al. (1996) and Zizi (1996) discuss a "visualization" approach to

Web browsing that is very similar to an approach described in the literature almost forty years ago (Doyle, 1961).

4.   Librarians should not be misled by the fact that software is available to aid the implementation of expert systems on the Web (Huntington, 1997). Except in a trivial application, the knowledge engineering investment needed will be very considerable.

5.   Almost 20 years ago, Clarke and Cronin (1983) suggested that an appropriate application of expert systems might be to catalog electronic publications as they are generated online. Jeng (1996) has recently presented a vision of cataloging for network resources, but her approach requires more human intellectual processing that automatic processing.

Appendix 1

Sample letter to vendors

F.W. Lancaster

1807 Cindy Lynn · Urbana, IL 61802 · (217) 384-7798 · Fax: (217) 244-3302

October 31, 2000

«Title»
«Company»
«Address1»
«Address2»
«City», «State» «PostalCode»

Dear Colleague:

I would be most grateful if you could send me full information on the following product:

«Product»

I would also like information on any of your other products that make use of artificial intelligence, expert systems, or related technologies.

I need this as input to a research project, funded by the Special Libraries Association, that is looking at potential applications of such technologies to the operations of special libraries.

Sincerely,

F.W. Lancaster
Professor Emeritus
University of Illinois

Appendix 2

Sample letter to authors

F.W. Lancaster

1807 Cindy Lynn · Urbana, IL 61802 · (217) 384-7798 · Fax: (217) 244-3302

October 31, 2000

«FirstName» «LastName»
«Company»
«Address1»
«Address2»
«City», «State» «PostalCode»
«Country»

Dear «Name»:

My colleague, Amy Warner, and I are working on a research project for the Special Libraries Association. The objective is to determine to what extent artificial intelligence, expert systems and related technologies are applicable to the operations of libraries in general, and special libraries in particular, now and in the immediate future.

Our search of the literature has disclosed that fact that you have worked on a system of possible interest to us, namely:

«Product»

We would be most grateful if you could help us in our project, first by answering the few questions on the attached sheet and, second, by sending us the latest information/publications/memoranda you have on the work. We are particularly interested in any unpublished reports you may be able to share with us, especially if such reports give details on why, if they are no longer active, the projects may have been discontinued.

If you wish to discuss this with me, I can be reached at 217/384-7798. Alternatively, you may send e-mail to Amy Warner at awarner@umich.edu. Please mail to the address on the letterhead.

Your help in this project would be very greatly appreciated.

Sincerely,

F.W. Lancaster
Professor Emeritus
University of Illinois

Appendix 3

Author questionnaire

Which of the following statements best describes the status of the project/system referred to in the letter?

❑ Existed as an idea on paper but never implemented in any form.

❑ An experimental system was established but has been discontinued.

❑ An experimental system still exists.

❑ A prototype was built but discontinued.

❑ A prototype system still exists.

❑ A fully operational system was implemented but has been discontinued.

❑ A fully operational system exists.

If the project/system has been discontinued, please indicate why. (Check all appropriate boxes.)

❑ Lack of funds.

❑ Too much effort was needed to keep it updated.

❑ Personnel responsible moved to different positions or assignments.

❑ System did not work as well as expected. Briefly explain:

❑ Other reason. Please explain:

If you would be willing to discuss this with us further, please let us know how you can be reached:
Telephone:
E-mail:

Appendix 4

Sources for keeping current with new developments in advanced technologies

The sources listed here will be useful in providing more details on the scope and application of the technologies discussed earlier in the book, and in keeping current with new developments in these technologies.

General surveys

Durkin, J. *Expert Systems: Catalog of Applications*. Akron, OH, Intelligent Computer Systems, Inc., 1993. (This is an excellent and comprehensive overview of applications in all fields, with bibliographic references, as of a few years ago.)

Hengl, T. *AI on the Internet*. Phoenix, AZ, Knowledge Technology, Inc., 1995. (Gives Internet addresses for sites providing information of various kinds on artificial intelligence or making AI programs available. However, this is now very much out-of-date because of the frequent changes in Internet addresses.)

Murch, R. and Johnson, T. *Intelligent Software Agents*. New York, Prentice-Hall, 1998. (A readable and comprehensive account of agent technology, how it works, and what its effects may be.)

Web sources of value include:

Artificial Intelligence Resources
http://ai.iit.nrc.ca/ai_top.html
(sponsored by the Canadian National Research Council)

Artificial Intelligence: WWW Virtual Library
  http://www.cs.reading.ac.uk/people/dwc/ai.html

American Association for Artificial Intelligence
  http://www.aaai.org

ACM SIGART
  http://sigart.acm.org

CMU Artificial Intelligence Repository
  http://www.cs.cmu.edu/Groups/AI/html/repository.html

Text Retrieval Conference Home Page
  http://trec.nist.gov

Message Understanding Conference (MUC) Proceedings
  http://www.muc.saic.com/proceedings/proceedings_index.html

Trade journals

The following journals all include information on new products
and/or articles discussing new developments in the field.

> *Computerworld*
> *Datamation*
> *Information Week*
> *InfoWorld*
> *Internet World*
> *MacWEEK*
> *Net Guide*
> *Network World*
> *PC AI*
> *PC Magazine*
> *PC World*
> *Web Week*

Scholarly journals

The trade journals are useful as sources of information on new products. However, the claims made in product announcements are often greatly exaggerated. Many of the articles in these sources are written by representatives of software producers and these, too, have to be taken with a grain of salt. More realistic surveys of new developments can be found in:

AI Magazine
Communications of the ACM
Data Mining and Knowledge Discovery
IEEE Expert
Expert Systems
Expert Systems with Applications
Intelligence
Internet Research

Appendix 5

Criteria for deciding when an expert system approach may be justified

Dreyfus and Dreyfus (1986) and Quantrille and Liu (1991) both give useful guidance on the types of applications for which expert system development may be justified. Their advice is included verbatim here. While they are dealing with fields quite distant from library science, many of the general principles are still applicable. Elofson (1995) gives advice on the application of knowledge engineering to "episodic classification problems"—situations too transient to justify a full expert systems approach. Also useful are a paper by Markus and Keil (1994), which discusses factors likely to affect the adoption of information systems in general and expert systems in particular in the corporate environment, and a discussion by Oravec and Travis (1992) on systems judged less than successful. King and McAulay (1991) conclude, perhaps somewhat surprisingly, that expert systems applied in management are more likely to succeed if based on "academic knowledge" than when based on knowledge gleaned from managers.

Dreyfus and Dreyfus (pp. 120-121)
(Reprinted with the permission of The Free Press, a division of Simon & Schuster, from *Mind Over Machine: the Power of Human Intuition and Expertise in the Era of the Computer*, by Hubert L. Dreyfus and Stuart E. Dreyfus. Copyright © 1986 by Hubert L. Dreyfus and Stuart E. Dreyfus.)

Those who are most acutely aware of the limitations of expert systems are best able to exploit their real capabilities. Dr. Sandra Cook, manager of the Financial Expert Systems Program at Sri International, is one of those enlightened practitioners. She cautions prospective clients that expert systems should not be expected to perform as well as human experts, nor should they be seen as simulations of human expert thinking. Cook lists eight reasonable conditions for successful applications (meaning that fairly high-quality performance can be made generally available within a company employing few if any true experts):

1. No algorithmic solution to the problem should exist, so that expertise is indeed required. (Recall that an algorithmic solution procedure is one that is guaranteed to find the demonstrably best solution to a problem.)

2. The problem can be satisfactorily solved by human experts at such a high level that somewhat inferior performance is still acceptable. (Stock market prediction, for example, would be an inappropriate area because human experts themselves perform erratically.)

3. There is a significant likelihood of a poor decision if made by a nonexpert. (Processing business credit applications is a reasonable area for expert system design, because inexperienced beginners have little ability to recognize nonroutine cases.)

4. Poor decisions must have significant impacts. (Experts systems are expensive to create and maintain.)

5. The problem must remain relatively unchanged during the time it takes a user of the system to solve the problem interactively. (Any expert system advice concerning the control of a nuclear reactor during a crisis would come too late to be of use. Only human experts or self-contained computer programs are fast enough to influence events.)

6. The knowledge domain must be relatively static. (Otherwise the system would require expensive continuous updating.)

7. A patient and cooperative expert must be available to the project to answer hypothetical questions which at best reveal the reasoning process he or she may once have used but has discarded since becoming an expert. This exercise can be frustrating, especially if the conclusion generated by the rules the expert articulates frequently fails to match his intuitive responses.

8. The political climate of the business must be conductive to the introduction of a new tool substituting certain user skills (such as furnishing information, sometimes judgemental, to a computer) for others (such as decision-making).

Quantrille and Liu (pp. 397-401)
(Reprinted by permission of Academic Press and Dr. Y. A. Liu)

16.2 Development of Expert Systems

Expert systems have received a lot of attention from the press in the 1980s. Unfortunately, much of the writing sensationalized the field. Expectations rose dramatically as some people, fueled by public speculation, began to over-promise. Misconceptions about what AI can and cannot do arose and they persist today. Many rushed into the field in search of quick answers and quick profits. Many AI researchers saw what was happening and feared a backlash once all the excitement wore off.

In 1988-90, things did begin to change. Some of the realities and limitations of AI techniques became evident. An AI backlash has resulted to a certain extent, but fortunately, it has not been wide-scale. Instead, the optimism remains, with a better sense of realism than before. Both the benefits and limitations are better appreciated.

When is an expert-system development warranted? This question must be answered before we initiate an expert-system project. D. Waterman (1986) gives some good guidelines on when we should consider using expert systems. Expert systems can be a very powerful asset. However, they also require significant investment in development cost. An expert system should be considered only when development is:

- Possible;

- Appropriate; and

- Justified.

The next sub-sections discuss what is meant by "possible," "appropriate," and "justified."

A. Identifying Expert-System Possibilities

Not all problems can be solved by expert systems. Before undertaking an expert-system project, we must identify the problem and project characteristics to ensure that an expert system is indeed possible. What are the characteristics of a problem that could possibly be solved using expert systems? Figure 16.1 summarizes the necessary requirements.

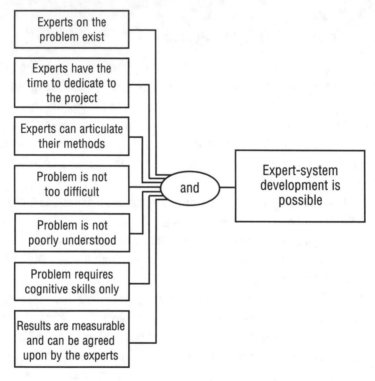

Figure 16.1   Necessary requirements for expert-system development

For a knowledge-based system to be possible, an expert on the field of application, called the *domain expert*, must exist. In addition, the expert must be able and willing to dedicate time to the project. Finally, the expert must have the ability to articulate his methods to the point where the *knowledge engineer* can correctly capture it into the knowledge base. The knowledge engineer is the

AI programmer who takes the problem, casts it into an AI framework, and programs the computer to achieve objectives.

Besides requiring the available human expertise, the nature of the problem also affects whether an expert system is possible or not. First, the problem cannot be too difficult; we must be able to characterize it in some way. Secondly, the problem must not be poorly understood, else the developed knowledge base will be inaccurate and unreliable. Third, the problem must require cognitive skills rather than physical skills. Expert systems are computer-based tools that cannot perform any physical activity. Note, however, that an expert system *can* be linked with something that does have physical skills. This happens frequently in robotics. Finally, the solution to the task at hand must be measurable and can be agreed upon by experts. This allows us to test and guide the expert-system development, and gives us a means of "quality control."

Note that in Figure 16.1, *all* of the defined criteria must be met for an expert system to be possible. If all the criteria are not fulfilled, we must seriously question if expert-system development is indeed possible. What is the most common pitfall in expert-system development? Underestimating the complexity of the problem. Thus, of all the criteria specified in Figure 16.1, there are two guidelines that we must consider carefully:

(1) The problem must not be too difficult; and

(2) The problem must not be poorly understood.

When an expert system fails its objectives, almost invariably one of these two criteria is violated. These criteria are violated because, at the beginning of the project, we tend to underestimate the complexity of the problem.

B. Determining the Appropriateness of Expert-System Development

Just because an expert system is possible, it may not be appropriate. Once we have identified an application that is possible, we need to determine if it is indeed appropriate to develop the system. This step can sometimes be the most difficult. Figure 16.2 shows the criteria on the appropriateness of an expert-system application.

Clearly, the problem must involve symbolic processing and the use of heuristics. If this is not the case, then mathematical modeling may be more appropriate. Another point to evaluate is how difficult the problem is. If the solution to the problem is too easy, another application, such as a sophisticated spreadsheet or database, may be better suited for the job.

Although the problem must be of sufficient complexity to utilize an expert system, it cannot be too complex. If the project is overly ambitious, it will get bogged down in the knowledge-engineering and prototyping stages. The knowledge base may "balloon" to an unmanageable size. The expert system may not run fast enough to be practical. People will lose interest, and the project may fail. Expectations can run high, so we must be careful in choosing a project with the right complexity.

For chemical engineering applications, how do we determine if an application is complex enough but not too complex? One rule of thumb we may use is that if it takes less two or three hours for an engineer to solve, the problem is too easy. If the problem takes more than two days, it is too difficult. Of course, this rule depends on the nature of the problem, and is a moving target. Computer-hardware improvements are steadily converting previously impossible tasks into possible ones. In addition, if the application is to be used repeatedly (as in chemical process design), it may pay to develop an expert system for the application.

We strongly recommend that *expert systems be developed on problems that allow the system to be prototyped rapidly* (in one to six months depending on the nature of the project and the business). A rapid prototype has two key advantages:

(1) Project momentum is maintained once the system is up and running.

(2) When developing the system, the following statement becomes acutely true:

> *You don't know what you don't know.*

What does this statement mean? We may think that we have the knowledge correctly characterized, but invariably, holes and contradictions in the knowledge appear. System development is therefore an evolutionary process. The sooner we get a prototype running, the sooner we can test and modify it to perform accurately in real-world situations.

Early prototyping allows the expert system to have practical impact as soon as possible. Without rapid prototyping, we could be waiting a long time for any results.

If a problem does not facilitate prototyping, it may not be an appropriate expert-system application. Typical problems that fall into this category are those requiring "perfect" performance. Expert systems use knowledge to enable computers to perform like human experts. If we use a human expert to solve a problem, there is no guarantee that this expert will be able to find an acceptable solution. The same is true for expert systems. If "perfect" performance is required, an algorithmic approach may be more appropriate.

As an example, let us consider an expert system designed to handle space-shuttle docking. Space-shuttle docking requires perfection; if we mess up, we may lose a life or a $700-million satellite. Space-shuttle docking control is not a good expert-system application. It is impossible to prototype the system correctly on the earth, and therefore the initial execution would probably be unreliable. Unfortunately, there is no "tweaking" it to improve the system performance after the system is placed into service; it must perform perfectly immediately after installation or disaster can result.

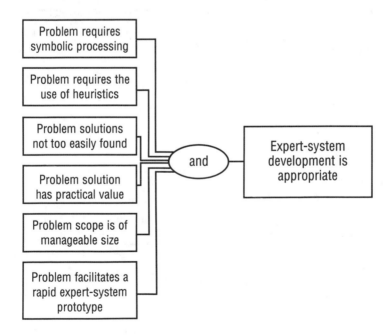

Figure 16.2 Evaluating the appropriateness of an expert-system application

C. Justifying Expert-System Development

Even though an expert-system approach is possible and appropriate, the project may not be justified. Expert systems require a significant investment of time and money. To justify an expert-system project, there must be a definite need with payback that outweighs the required investment. Figure 16.3 shows some of these needs that justify the expert-system development.

Some of the primary justifications of the expert-system development relate to solving the problem at hand. Expert systems are justified when:

(1) solution of a single problem has a high payoff (such as in oil exploration); or

(2) solution of a complex problem rapidly and repetitively will enhance pro-
ductivity (such as in chemical process design).

Other justifications also exist. If human expertise is going to be lost, is generally unavailable, or is needed in multiple locations, then the expert-system development is justified. An example is fault diagnosis, where during a critical malfunc-
tion in a plant, the process expert may not be available on-site.

Note that Figure 16.3 is not all-inclusive. The figure is meant to display some of the more common justifications for expert-system development. A specific problem may have a unique justification of its own.

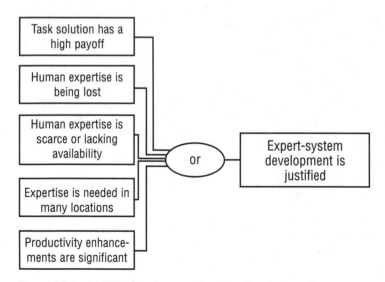

Figure 16.3   Justifications for expert-system developement

To summarize, we must make sure that an expert system is possible, appropriate, and justified before starting a project. A number of classifications of problems in chemical engineering have been found to be appropriate for the expert-system development, as mentioned in section 16.1. These application areas are:

- Fault diagnosis

- Process control

- Process design

- Planning and operations

- Modeling and simulation

- Product development

We discuss these applications in the following sections. Note that we *do not* present an exhaustive discussion of every published paper. We only highlight representative works. However, we have made an attempt to include essentially as many chemical engineering publications as possible up to early 1991 as references for further reading.

References and Further Reading

Harmon, P. and D. King, *Expert Systems: Artificial Intelligence in Business,* John Wiley & Sons, New York, NY (1985).

Hayes-Roth, F., D. A. Waterman and D. B. Lenat, *Building Expert Systems,* pp. 3-29, Addison Wesley, Reading, MA (1983).

Jackson, P., *Introduction to Expert Systems,* Addison-Wesley, Reading, MA (1986).

Pierce, T. H. and B. A. Hohne (Eds.), *Artificial Intelligence Applications in Chemistry,* ACS Symposium Series, 306, American Chemical Society, Washington, DC (1986).

Waterman, D. A., *A Guide to Expert Systems,* pp. 135-161, Addison Wesley, Reading, MA (1986).

References

Acorn, T. L. and Walden, S. H. SMART: support management automated reasoning technology for Compaq customer service. In: *Innovative Applications of Artificial Intelligence 4*; ed. by A. C. Scott and P. Klahr, pp. 3-18. Cambridge, MA, MIT Press, 1992.

Agnew, B. et al. Multi-media indexing over the Web. In: *Storage and Retrieval for Image and Video Databases V*; ed. by I. K. Sethi and R. C. Jain, pp. 72-83. Bellingham, WA, International Society for Optical Engineering, 1997.

Alberico, R. and Micco, M. *Expert Systems for Reference and Information Retrieval*. Westport, CT, Meckler, 1990.

Allaërt, F. A. and Dusserre, L. Decision support system and medical liability. In: (Proceedings of the) *Sixteenth Annual Symposium on Computer Applications in Medical Care*, pp. 750-753. New York, McGraw Hill, 1993.

Allen, B. P. Case-based reasoning: business applications. *Communications of the ACM*, 37(3), 1994, 40-42.

Allen, R. B. User models: theory, method and practice. *International Journal of Man-Machine Studies*, 32(5), 1990, 511-543.

Alleva, F. et al. Can continuous speech recognizers handle isolated speech? *Speech Communication*, 26, 1998, 183-189.

Anand, T. and Kahn, G. Focusing knowledge-based techniques on market analysis. *IEEE Expert*, 8(4), 1993, 19-24.

Anand, T. and Kahn, G. Making sense of gigabytes: a system for knowledge-based market analysis. In: *Innovative Applications of Artificial Intelligence 4*; ed. by A. C. Scott and P. Klahr, pp. 57-69. Cambridge, MA, MIT Press, 1992.

Andersen, P. M. et al. Automatic extraction of facts from press releases to generate news stories. In: *Proceedings of the Third Conference on*

Applied Natural Language Processing, pp. 170-177. San Francisco, Morgan Kaufmann, 1992.

Andrews, D. Self-help software to the rescue. *Byte*, 21(10), 1996, 26-27.

Anick, P. G. Integrating natural language processing and information retrieval in a troubleshooting help desk. *IEEE Expert*, 8(6), 1993, 9-17.

Atkinson, R. Library functions, scholarly communication, and the foundation of the digital library: laying claim to the control zone. *Library Quarterly*, 66, 1996, 239-265.

Atkinson, R. Networks, hypertext, and academic information services: some longer-range implications. *College & Research Libraries*, 54, 1993, 199-215.

Atkinson, R. Text mutability and collection administration. *Library Acquisitions: Practice and Theory*, 14, 1990, 355-358.

Ayres, F. H. et al. *QUALCAT: Automation of Quality Control in Cataloguing*. Boston Spa, British Library, 1994. R&D Report 6068.

Backus, J. Personal communication, October 28, 1996.

Baeza-Yates, R. and Ribeiro-Neto, B. *Modern Information Retrieval*. Reading, MA, Addison-Wesley, 1999.

Bailey, C. W., Jr. The Intelligent Reference Information System project: a merger of CD-ROM LAN and expert system technologies. *Information Technology and Libraries*, 11, 1992, 237-244.

Bailey, C. W., Jr. and Myers, J. E. *Expert Systems in ARL Libraries*. Washington, DC, Association of Research Libraries, 1991.

Bailin, S. et al. Application of machine learning to the organization of institutional software repositories. *Telematics and Informatics*, 10, 1993, 283-299.

Bainbridge, D. I. Computer-aided diagnosis and negligence. *Medicine, Science and the Law*, 31(2), 1991, 127-136.

Bainbridge, D. I. Expert systems in law: practice and promise. *International Journal of Applied Expert Systems*, 1(1), 1993, 25-40.

Balas, E. A. et al. An expert system for performance-based direct delivery of published clinical evidence. *Journal of the American Medical Informatics Association*, 3(1), 1996, 56-65.

Banerjee, K. Is data mining right for your library? *Computers in Libraries*, 18 (10), 1998, 28-31.

Banks, M. A. Using AltaVista's translation assistant: the popular search engine translates text on Web pages to or from English and five other languages. *Link-Up*, 15 (4), 1998, 26.

Basden, A. Three levels of benefits in expert systems. *Expert Systems*, 11(2), 1994, 99-107.

Bassøe, C. F. Automated diagnoses from clinical narratives: a medical system based on computerized medical records, natural language processing, and neural network technology. *Neural Networks*, 8, 1995, 313-319.

Bateman, J. and Teich, E. Selective information presentation in an integrated publication system: an application of genre-driven text generation. *Information Processing & Management*, 31, 1995, 753-767.

Bates, M. J. Where should the person stop and the information search interface start? *Information Processing & Management*, 26, 1990, 575-591.

Benford, S. et al. Visualising and populating the Web: collaborative virtual environments for browsing, searching and inhabiting Webspace. *Computer Networks and ISDN Systems*, 29, 1997, 1751-1761.

Bennett, J. L. On-line access to information: NSF as an aid to the indexer/cataloger. *American Documentation*, 20, 1969, 213-220.

Bennett, J. L. et al. *Observing and Evaluating an Interactive Process: a Pilot Experiment in Indexing*. San Jose, CA, IBM Research Laboratory, 1972.

Benois-Pineau, J. et al. Query by synthesized sketch in an architectural database. In: *Storage and Retrieval for Image and Video Databases V*; ed. by I. K. Sethi and R. C. Jain, pp. 361-367. Bellingham, WA, International Society for Optical Engineering, 1997.

Berner, E. S., ed. *Clinical Decision Support Systems: Theory and Practice*, New York, Springer, 1999.

Berner, E. S. et al. Performance of four computer-based diagnostic systems. *New England Journal of Medicine*, 330, 1994, 1792-1796.

Bianchi, G. and Giorgi, M. Towards an expert system as intelligent assistant for the design of an online documentation service. In: *Proceedings of the Tenth International Online Information Meeting*, pp. 199-208. Oxford, Learned Information, 1986.

Blair, D. C. and Maron, M. E. An evaluation of retrieval effectiveness for a full-text document retrieval system. *Communications of the ACM*, 28 (3), 1985, 289-299.

Blake, P. Information agents. *Online & CDROM Review*, 18, 1994, 189-190.

Blanchard, D. Agents infiltrate the business world. *PC AI*, 10 (4), 1996, 39-42.

Blum, T. et al. Audio databases with content-based retrieval. In: *Intelligent Multimedia Information Retrieval*; ed. by M. T. Maybury, pp. 113-135. Menlo Park, CA, AAAI Press, 1997.

Bocionek, S. R. Agent systems that negotiate and learn. *International Journal of Human-Computer Studies*, 42, 1995, 265-288.

Bock, G. Search '97 from Verity: making text retrieval an application. *Snap Shots*, 3(9), September 1996. (*Snap Shots* is a monthly newsletter produced by the Patricia Seybold Group.)

Borgman, C. L. and Plute, Y. I. User models for information systems: prospects and problems. In: *Artificial Intelligence and Expert Systems: Will They Change the Library?*; ed. by F. W. Lancaster and L. C. Smith, pp. 178-193. Urbana-Champaign, University of Illinois, Graduate School of Library and Information Science, 1992.

Borman, S. Electronic laboratory notebooks may revolutionize research record keeping. *Chemical & Engineering News*, 72, May 23, 1994, 10-12, 16, 18-19.

Borst, F. et al. TEXTINFO: a tool for automatic determination of patient clinical profiles using text analysis. In: *Assessing the Value of Medical Informatics: Fifteenth Annual Symposium on Computer Applications in Medical Care*; ed. by P. D. Clayton, pp. 63-67. New York, McGraw Hill, 1992.

Bosman, F. et al. CoBRA/RUG: expert system for user queries. In: *Knowledge Organization and Quality Management*; ed. by H. Albrechtsen and S. Oernager, pp. 304-311. Frankfurt, Indeks Verlag, 1994.

Brachman, R. J. et al. Mining business databases. *Communications of the ACM*, 39 (11), 1996, 42-48.

Bradley, P. Intelligent agents on the Web. *Managing Information*, 6 (1), 1999, 35-9, 41.

Brajnik, G. G. et al. User modeling in expert man-machine interfaces: a case study in intelligent information retrieval. *IEEE Transactions on Systems, Man, and Cybernetics*, 20, 1990, 166-185.

Bramer, M. A. Introduction. In: *Research and Development in Expert Systems IX*; ed. by M. A. Bramer and R. W. Milne, pages 1-4. Cambridge, Cambridge University Press, 1993.

Bramer, M. A. and Milne, R. W., eds. *Research and Development in Expert Systems IX*. Cambridge, Cambridge University Press, 1993.

Brandow, R. et al. Automatic condensation of electronic publications by sentence selection. *Information Processing & Management*, 31, 1995, 675-685.

Brin, B. and Cochran, E. Access and ownership in the academic environment: one library's progress report. *Journal of Academic Librarianship*, 20, 1994, 207-212.

Brown, L. C. B. An expert system for predicting approval plan receipts. *Library Acquisitions: Practice & Theory*, 17, 1993, 155-164.

Buckland, M. K. and Florian, D. Expertise, task complexity, and artificial intelligence: a conceptual framework. *Journal of the American Society for Information Science*, 42, 1991, 635-643.

Burger, F. et al. Managing structured documents in distributed publishing environments. In: *Database and Expert Systems Applications*; ed. by D. Karagiannis, pp. 83-92. Berlin, Springer-Verlag, 1994. (Lecture Notes in Computer Science, Volume 856).

Burke, R. et al. Intelligent Web search engines. *PC AI*, 11(1), 1997, 39-42.

Buxton, A. B. A quantitative evaluation of Infosearch multi-host access (Easynet). In: *Online Information 88*. Volume 2, pp. 715-722. Oxford, Learned Information, 1988.

Byun, D. H. and Suh, E. H. Human resource management expert systems technology. *Expert Systems*, 11(2), 1994, 109-119.

Cass, O. W. Automated speech technology for gastrointestinal endoscopy reporting and image recording. In: *Assessing the Value of Medical Informatics: Fifteenth Annual Symposium on Computer Applications in Medical Care*; ed. by P. D. Clayton, pp. 968-969. New York, McGraw Hill, 1992.

Cawkell, T. Tracking fast-moving technology: the progress of speech recognition. *Journal of Information Science*, 25 (1), 1999, 79-84.

Chan, L. L. and Carande, R. J. Public health—in search of a knowledge domain and expert reference advisory system. *Bulletin of the Medical Library Association*, 79, 1991, 178-181.

Chandler, P. G. et al. An expert system to aid cataloging and searching electronic documents on digital libraries. *Expert Systems with Applications*, 12, 1997, 405-416.

Chang, K. H. et al. A self-improving help desk service system using case-based reasoning techniques. *Computers in Industry*, 30, 1996, 113-125.

Chang, P. L. et al. Clinical evaluation of a renal mass diagnostic expert system. *Computers in Biology and Medicine*, 24, 1994, 315-322.

Charniak, E. Natural language learning. *ACM Computing Surveys*, 27, 1995, 317-319.

Chen, H. Semantic research for digital libraries. *D-Lib Magazine*, 5(10), 1999, http://mirrored.ukoln.ac.uk/lis-journals/dlib/dlib/october99/chen/10chen.html

Chen, H. et al. Automatic concept classification of text from electronic meetings. *Communications of the ACM*, 37(10), 1994, 56-73.

Chen, H. et al. Automatic thesaurus generation for an electronic community system. *Journal of the American Society for Information Science*, 46, 1995, 175-193.

Chen, H. et al. Internet categorization and search: a self-organizing approach. *Journal of Visual Communication and Image Representation*, 7(1), 1996, 88-102.

Chen, H. et al. An intelligent personal spider (agent) for dynamic Internet/Intranet searching. *Decision Support Systems*, 23, 1998a, 41-58.

Chen, H. et al. Internet browsing and searching: user evaluations of category map and concept space techniques. *Journal of the American Society for Information Science*, 49, 1998b, 582-603.

Chen, H. et al. Semantic indexing and searching using a Hopfield net. *Journal of Information Science*, 24 (1), 1998c, 3-18.

Chen, H. et al. A smart itsy-bitsy spider for the Web. *Journal of the American Society for Information Science*, 49, 1998d, 604-618.

Chen, Z. Let documents talk to each other: a computer model for connection of short documents. *Journal of Documentation*, 49, 1993, 44-54.

Chinchor, N. MUC-7 information extraction task definition. *MUC-7 Proceedings*, 1998, http://www.muc.saic.com/proceedings/proceedings/index.html

Cho, W. et al. Expert-system technology for hotels: concierge application. *Cornell Hotel and Restaurant Administration Quarterly*, 37, 1996, 54-60.

Choi, Y. S. et al. Hierarchically organized neural net agents for distributed Web information retrieval. In: *Proceedings of the Twenty-Third Annual International Computer Software and Applications Conference*, pp. 192-197. Los Alamitos, CA, IEEE Computer Society, 1999.

Chu, H. and Rosenthal, M. Search engines for the World Wide Web: a comparative study and evaluation methodology. *Proceedings of the American Society for Information Science*, 33, 1996, 127-135.

Chung, Y. M. et al. Automatic indexing using an associative neural network. In: *Proceedings of the 3rd ACM Conference on Digital Libraries*, pp. 59-66. New York, Association for Computing Machinery, 1998.

Church, K. W. and Rau, L. F. Commercial applications of natural language processing. *Communications of the ACM*, 38(11), 1995, 71-79.

Clarke, A. and Cronin, B. Expert systems and library/information work. *Journal of Librarianship*, 15, 1983, 277-292.

Coiera, E. W. Artificial intelligence in medicine: the challenges ahead. *Journal of the American Medical Informatics Association*, 3, 1996, 363-365.

Conte, R., Jr. Guiding lights. *Internet World*, 7(5), 1996, 41-44.

Cosgrove, S. J. and Weimann, J. M. Expert system technology applied to item classification. *Library Hi Tech*, 10(1/2), 1992, 33-40.

Coult G. Intelligent agents. *Managing Information*, 6 (1), 1999, 33-34.

Cowie, J. and Lehnert, W. Information extraction. *Communications of the ACM*, 39(1), 1996, 80-91.

Croft, W. B. What do people want from information retrieval? (The top 10 research issues for companies that use and sell IR systems). *D-Lib Magazine*, 1995 November.
http://www.dlib.org/dlib/november95/11croft.html

Croft, W. B. and Turtle, H. R. Text retrieval and inference. In: *Text-Based Intelligent Systems*; ed. by P. S. Jacobs, pp. 127-155. Hillsdale, NJ, Lawrence Erlbaum, 1992.

Cromp, R. F. and Dorfman, E. A spatial data handling system for retrieval of images by unrestricted regions of user interest. *Telematics and Informatics*, 9, 1992, 221-241.

Dabke, K. P. and Thomas, K. Expert system guidance for library users. *Library Hi Tech*, 10 (1/2), 1992, 53-60.

Dale, R. et al. Dynamic document delivery: generating natural language texts on demand. In: *Proceedings of the Ninth International Workshop on Database and Expert Systems Applications*, pp. 131-136. Los Alamitos, CA, IEEE Computer Society, 1998.

Daniel, M. et al. CADIAG-2 and MYCIN-like systems. *Artificial Intelligence in Medicine*, 9, 1997, 241-259.

Danilewitz, D. B. and Freiheit, F. E., IV. A knowledge-based system within a cooperative processing environment. In: *Innovative Applications of Artificial Intelligence 4*; ed. by A. C. Scott and P. Klahr, pp. 19-36. Cambridge, MA, MIT Press, 1992.

David, A. A. and Bueno, D. User modeling and cooperative information retrieval in information retrieval systems. *Knowledge Organization*, 26 (1), 1999, 30-45.

Davies, R. Expert systems and cataloguing. In: *The Application of Expert Systems in Libraries and Information Centres*; ed. by A. Morris, pp. 133-166. New York, Bowker-Saur, 1992.

Davis, C. et al. Chirico—a framework for computerization of medical practice guidelines. In: *Proceedings* (of the) *Seventh International Conference on Tools With Artificial Intelligence*, pp. 224-227. Los Alamitos, CA, IEEE Computer Society Press, 1995.

DeBrower, A. M. and Jones, D. T. Application of an expert system to collection development: donation processing in a special library. *Library Software Review*, 10(6), 1991, 384-389.

Delmonico, D. Extracting gold. *CommunicationsWeek*, number 596, February 12, 1996, 43-44.

Demas, S. et al. The Internet and collection development: main-streaming selection of Internet resources. *Library Resources & Technical Services*, 39, 1995, 275-290.

Demasco, P. W. and McCoy, K. F. Generating text from compressed input: an intelligent interface for people with severe motor impairments. *Communications of the ACM*, 35 (5), 1992, 68-78.

Denning, R. and Smith, P. J. Interface design concepts in the development of ELSA, an intelligent electronic library search assistant. *Information Technology and Libraries*, 13, 1994, 133-147.

Desai, B. C. Supporting discovery in virtual libraries. *Journal of the American Society for Information Science*, 48, 1997, 190-204.

Desai, B. C. et al. CINDI: a virtual library indexing and discovery system. *Library Trends*, 48, 1999, 209-233.

Diamond, L. W. et al. Are normative expert systems appropriate for diagnostic pathology? *Journal of the American Medical Informatics Association*, 2(2), 1995, 85-93.

Di Loreto, F. et al. A visual object-oriented query language for geographic information systems. In: *Database and Expert Systems Applications*; ed. by N. Revell and A. M. Tjoa, pp. 103-113. Berlin, Springer-Verlag, 1995. (Lecture Notes in Computer Science, Number 978).

Ding, W. and Marchionini, G. A comparative study of Web search service performance. *Proceedings of the American Society for Information Science*, 33, 1996, 136-142.

Dong, X. and Su, L. T. Search engines on the World Wide Web and information retrieval from the Internet: a review and evaluation. *Online & CDROM Review*, 21(2), 1997, 67-82.

Doyle, L. B. Semantic road maps for literature searchers. *Journal of the Association for Computing Machinery*, 8, 1961, 553-578.

Drabenstott, K. M. *Analytical Review of the Library of the Future.* Washington, DC, Council on Library Resources, 1994.

Drenth, H. et al. Expert systems as information intermediaries. *Annual Review of Information Science and Technology*, 26, 1991, 113-154.

Dreyfus, H. L. and Dreyfus, S. E. *Mind Over Machine: The Power of Human Intuition and Expertise in the Era of the Computer.* New York, Free Press, 1986.

Driscoll, J. R. et al. The operation and performance of an artificially intelligent keywording system. *Information Processing & Management*, 27, 1991, 43-54.

Duffy, G. and Tucker, S. A. Political science: artificial intelligence applications. *Social Science Computer Review*, 13(1), 1995, 1-20.

Durkin, J. *Expert Systems: Catalog of Applications.* Akron, OH, Intelligent Computer Systems, 1993.

Dwinnell, W. Text mining: dealing with unstructured data. *PC AI*, 13 (3), 1999, 20-23.

Eberts, R. and Habibi, S. Neural network-based agents for integrating information for production systems. *International Journal of Production Economics*, 38, 1995, 73-84.

Edelstein, H. Mining data warehouses. *Information Week*, Number 561, January 8, 1996, 48-51.

Edmonds, E. A. Support for collaborative design: agents and emergence. *Communications of the ACM*, 37(7), 1994, 41-47.

Efthimiadis, E. N. Online searching aids: a review of front ends, gateways and other interfaces. *Journal of Documentation*, 46, 1991, 218-262.

Efthimiadis, E. N. Query expansion. *Annual Review of Information Science and Technology*, 31, 1996, 121-187.

Eggert, A. A. et al. Converting chemical formulas to names: an expert strategy. *Journal of Chemical Information and Computer Sciences,* 32, 1992, 227-233.

Eggert, A. A. et al. Converting chemical names to formulas: a second expert problem. *Journal of Chemical Information and Computer Sciences,* 33, 1993, 458-465.

Eichmann, D. Ethical Web agents. *Computer Networks and ISDN Systems,* 28, 1995, 127-136.

Elofson, G. Intelligent agents extend knowledge-based systems feasibility. *IBM Systems Journal,* 34(1), 1995, 78-95.

Engle, R. L., Jr. Attempts to use computers as diagnostic aids in medical decision making: a thirty-year experience. *Perspectives in Biology and Medicine,* 35, 1992, 207-219.

Ennals, R. and Gardin, J. C., eds. *Interpretation in the Humanities: Perspectives from Artificial Intelligence.* London, British Library, 1990. Library and Information Research Report 71.

Ercegovac, Z. A multiple-observation approach in knowledge acquisition for expert systems: a case study. *Journal of the American Society for Information Science,* 43, 1992, 506-517.

Ercegovac, Z. and Borko, H. Design and implementation of an experimental cataloging advisor—Mapper. *Information Processing & Management,* 28, 1992a, 241-257.

Ercegovac, Z. and Borko, H. Performance evaluation of Mapper. *Information Processing & Management,* 28, 1992b, 259-268.

Etzioni, O. The World-Wide Web: quagmire or gold mine? *Communications of the ACM,* 39 (11), 1996, 65-68.

Etzioni, O. and Weld, D. A softbot-based interface to the Internet. *Communications of the ACM,* 37(7), 1994, 72-76.

Fayyad, U. et al. The KDD process for extracting useful knowledge from volumes of data. *Communications of the ACM,* 39 (11), 1996, 27-34.

Feder, J. D. and Hobbs, E. T. Speech recognition and full-text retrieval: interface and integration. *Proceedings of the Sixteenth National Online Meeting*, pp. 97-104. Medford, NJ, Learned Information, 1995.

Feifer, R. G. and Tazbaz, D. Interface design principles for interactive multimedia. *Telematics and Informatics*, 14, 1997, 51-65.

Feiten, B. and Günzel, S. Automatic indexing of a sound database using self-organizing neural nets. *Computer Music Journal*, 18(3), 1994, 53-65.

Feldman, S. The answer machine. *Searcher*, 8 (1), 2000a, 58-78.

Feldman, S. E. Manning & Napier Information Services announces CINDOR, a multi-language search-and-retrieval system. *Information Today*, 17 (2), 2000b, 42.

Feldman, S. E. NLP meets the jabberwocky: natural language processing in information retrieval. *Online*, 23(3), 1999, 62-72.

Feldman, S. E. Search Engine Watch: an outstanding and useful meta site. *Online*, 21(6), 1997, 62.

Feldman, S. E. and Yu, E. Intelligent agents: a primer. *Searcher*, 7 (9), 1999, 42-55.

Fellbaum, C., ed. *Wordnet: An Electronic Lexical Database.* Cambridge, MA, MIT Press, 1998.

Fenly, C. Technical services processes as models for assessing expert system suitability and benefits. In: *Artificial Intelligence and Expert Systems: Will They Change the Library?*; ed. by F. W. Lancaster and L. C. Smith, pp. 50-66. Urbana-Champaign, University of Illinois, Graduate School of Library and Information Science, 1992.

Ferri, F. et al. Intelligent management of epidemiologic data. In: *Assessing the Value of Medical Informatics: Fifteenth Annual Symposium on Computer Applications in Medical Care*; ed. by P. D. Clayton, pp. 343-347. New York, McGraw Hill, 1992.

Flickner, M. et al. Query by image and video content: the QBIC system. *Computer*, 28(9), 1995, 23-32.

Floridi, L. Brave.Net.World: the Internet as a disinformation superhighway? *Electronic Library*, 14, 1996, 509-514.

Flynn, M. K. Take a letter, computer: speech recognition is coming of age. *PC Magazine*, 12(13), 1993, 29.

Fontaine, T. and Shastri, L. A hybrid system for handprinted word recognition. In: *Proceedings of the Ninth Conference on Artificial Intelligence for Applications*, pp. 227-234. Los Alamitos, CA, IEEE Computer Society Press, 1993.

Foo, S. et al. An integrated help desk support for customer services over the World Wide Web—a case study. *Computers in Industry*, 41, 2000, 129-145.

Foote, J. An overview of audio information retrieval. *Multimedia Systems*, 7, 1999, 2-10.

Forslund, G. Toward cooperative advice-giving systems. *IEEE Expert*, 10 (4), 1995, 56-62.

Forsyth, D. A. Computer vision tools for finding images and video sequences. *Library Trends*, 48, 1999, 326-355.

Fowler, R. H. et al. Visualizing and browsing WWW semantic content. In: *Proceedings of the First Annual Conference on Emerging Technologies and Applications in Communications*, pp. 110-113. Los Alamitos, CA, IEEE Computer Society Press, 1996.

Fox, K. L. et al. SENTINEL: a multiple engine information retrieval and visualization system. *Journal of the American Society for Information Science*, 50, 1999, 616-625.

Fragoudis, D. and Likothanassis, S. D. Learning to identify interesting links in intelligent information discovery. In: *Proceedings of the 11th International Conference on Tools with Artificial Intelligence*, pp. 410-413. Los Alamitos, CA, IEEE Computer Society, 1999.

Frakes, W. B. and Baeza-Yates, R. *Information Retrieval: Data Structures & Algorithms*. Englewood Cliffs, NJ, Prentice Hall, 1992.

France, M. Smart contracts. *Forbes*, 154, August 29, 1994, supp. ASAP, 117-118.

Franz, M. and McCarley, J. S. Machine translation and monolingual information retrieval. In: *Proceedings of the 22nd Annual International Conference on Research and Development in Information Retrieval*, pp. 295-296. New York, ACM, 1999.

Friis, T. Assisted Indexing (CAIN). *IAALD Quarterly Bulletin*, 37 (1/2), 1992, 35-37.

Gao, Y. J. et al. Fuzzy multilinkage thesaurus builder in multimedia information systems. In: *Proceedings of Third International Conference on Document Analysis and Recognition*. Volume 1, pp. 142-145. Los Alamitos, CA, IEEE Computer Society Press, 1995.

Gerber, B. ORFEO: an expert reference advisor for opera. *Library Software Review*, 11, May/June 1992, 8-12.

Goldstein, J. et al. Summarizing text documents: sentence selection and evaluation metrics. In: *Proceedings of the 22nd Annual International Conference on Research and Development in Information Retrieval*, pp. 121-128. New York, ACM, 1999.

Goodman, M. Prism: a case-based telex classifier. In: *Innovative Applications of Artificial Intelligence 2*; ed. by A. Rappaport and R. Smith, pp. 25-37. Cambridge, MA, MIT Press, 1991.

Gowtham, M. S. and Kamat, S. K. An expert system as a tool to classification. *Library Science with a Slant to Documentation and Information Studies*, 32(2), 1995, 57-63.

Green, B. F. et al. BASEBALL: an automatic question-answerer. In: *Computers and Thought*; ed. by E. Feigenbaum and J. Feldman, pp. 207-216. New York, McGraw Hill, 1963.

Greene, R. J. and Hield, C. W. Data exploration systems for databases. *Telematics and Informatics*, 9, 1992, 255-269.

Grefenstette, G. Problems and approaches to cross language information retrieval. In: *Proceedings of the American Society for Information Science*, 35, 1998, 143-152.

Grimson, W. E. L. and Mundy, J. L. Computer vision applications. *Communications of the ACM*, 37 (3), 1994, 45-51.

Griswold, S. D. Unleashing agents. *Internet World*, 7(5), 1996, 55-57.

Grudin, J. and Palen, L. Emerging groupware successes in major corporations: studies of adoption and adaptation. In: *International Conference on Worldwide Computing and Its Applications*, pp. 142-153. Berlin, Springer-Verlag, 1997.

Gudivada, V. N. and Raghavan, V. V. Content-based image retrieval systems. *Computer*, 28(9), 1995, 18-22.

Gunter, B. Data mining: mother lode or fool's gold? *Quality Progress*, 29(4), 1996, 113-115, 117-118.

Guyette, L. et al. A rule-based expert system approach to class scheduling. *Computers and Electrical Engineering*, 20(2), 1994, 151-162.

Haas, S. W. Natural language processing: toward large-scale robust systems. *Annual Review of Information Science and Technology*, 31, 1996, 83-119.

Hall, G. S. Improving library performance: experimenting with expert systems. In: *Libraries: the Heart of the Matter*, pp. 126-130. Deakin, ACT, Australian Library and Information Association, 1992.

Hammond, K. et al. FAQ Finder: a case-based approach to knowledge navigation. In: *Proceedings* (of) *the 11th Conference on Artificial Intelligence for Applications*, pp. 80-86. Los Alamitos, CA, IEEE Computer Society Press, 1995.

Hanne, D. A discussion of knowledge-based systems and librarians: with a selected bibliography from library science and other disciplines. *Public Library Quarterly*, 16 (2), 1997, 20-44.

Hardy, I. T. Creating an expert system for legislative history research: Project CLEAR's "Lexpert". *Law Library Journal*, 85, 1993, 239-273.

Harley, B. L. and Knobloch, P. J. Government Documents Reference Aid: an expert system development project. *Government Publications Review*, 18(1), 1991, 15-34.

Harman, D. Overview of the first TREC conference. In: *SIGIR '93: Proceedings of the Sixteenth Annual International ACM SIGIR Conference on Research and Development in Information Retrieval*, pp. 36-47. New York, Association for Computing Machinery, 1993a.

Harman, D. User-friendly systems instead of user-friendly front-ends. *Journal of the American Society for Information Science*, 43, 1992, 164-174.

Harman, D., ed. *The First Text REtrieval Conference (TREC-1)*. Gaithersburg, MD, National Institute of Standards and Technology, 1993b. (NIST Special Publication 500-207).

Harris, R. Information technology and the de-skilling of librarians. *Computers in Libraries*, 12(1), 1992, 8-16.

Hart, P. E. and Graham, J. Query-free information retrieval. *IEEE Expert*, 12(5), 1997, 32-37.

Hartley, R. J. et al. The use of an expert system shell to provide legal advice to social workers in rural areas: experience with the Mental Health Act. *Online Information 91*; ed. by D. I. Raitt, pp. 435-443. Oxford, Learned Information, 1991.

Haug, P. and Beesley, D. Automated selection of clinical data to support radiographic interpretation. In: *Assessing the Value of Medical Informatics: Fifteenth Annual Symposium on Computer Applications in Medical Care*; ed. by P. D. Clayton, pp. 593-597. New York, McGraw Hill, 1992.

Hauptmann, A. G. Speech recognition in the Informedia digital video library: uses and limitations. In: *Proceedings (of the) Seventh International Conference on Tools With Artificial Intelligence*, pp. 288-294. Los Alamitos, CA, IEEE Computer Society Press, 1995.

Hauptmann, A. G. and Wactlar, H. D. Indexing and search of multi-modal information. In: *1997 IEEE International Conference on Acoustics, Speech, and Signal Processing*, pp. 195-198. Los Alamitos, CA, IEEE Computer Society, 1997.

Hauptmann, A. G. and Witbrock, M. J. Informedia: news-on-demand multimedia information acquisition and retrieval. In: *Intelligent Multimedia Information Retrieval*; ed. by M. T. Maybury, pp. 215-239. Menlo Park, CA, AAAI Press, 1997.

Haverkamp, D. and Gauch, S. Intelligent information agents: review and challenges for distributed information sources. *Journal of the American Society for Information Science*, 49, 1998, 304-311.

Hawks, C. P. Expert systems in technical services and collection management. *Information Technology and Libraries*, 13, 1994, 203-212.

Hayes, P. J. Intelligent high-volume text processing using shallow, domain-specific techniques. In: *Text-Based Intelligent Systems*; ed. by P. S. Jacobs, pp. 227-241. Hillsdale, NJ, Lawrence Erlbaum, 1992.

Hayes, P. J. and Koerner, G. Intelligent text technologies and their successful use by the information industry. In: *Proceedings* (of the) *14th National Online Meeting*, pp. 189-196. Medford, NJ, Learned Information, 1993.

Hayes, P. J. and Weinstein, S. P. Construe-TIS: a system for content-based indexing of a database of news stories. In: *Innovative Applications of Artificial Intelligence 2*; ed. by A. Rappaport and R. Smith, pp. 51-64. Cambridge, MA, MIT Press, 1991.

Hayes-Roth, F. and Jacobstein, N. The state of knowledge-based systems. *Communications of the ACM*, 37(3), 1994, 27-39.

Head, A. J. A question of interface design: how do online service GUIs measure up? *Online*, 21(3), 1997, 20-29.

Heathfield, H. The rise and 'fall' of expert systems in medicine. *Expert Systems*, 16 (3), 1999, 183-188.

Heidorn, P. B. Image retrieval as linguistic and nonlinguistic visual model matching. *Library Trends*, 48, 1999, 303-325.

Hirschman, L. The evolution of evaluation: lessons from the Message Understanding Conferences. *Computer Speech and Language*, 12, 1998, 281-305.

Hjerppe, R. and Olander, B. Cataloging and expert systems: AACR2 as a knowledge base. *Journal of the American Society for Information Science*, 40, 1989, 27-44.

Hobbs, J. R. et al. Robust processing of real-world natural-language texts. In: *Text-Based Intelligent Systems*; ed. by P. S. Jacobs, pp. 13-33. Hillsdale, NJ, Lawrence Erlbaum, 1992.

Holt, B. and Hartwick, L. 'Quick, who painted fish?': searching a picture database with the QBIC project at UC Davis. *Information Services & Use*, 14, 1994, 79-90.

Holt, B. et al. The QBIC project in the Department of Art and Art History at UC Davis. *Proceedings of the American Society for Information Science*, 34, 1997, 189-195.

Holzberg, C. S. At your service: custom news services track the topics you specify. *Internet World*, 7(5), 1996, 46-50, 52.

Horton, F. W., Jr. Human capital investment: key to the information age. *Information and Records Management*, 16(7), 1982, 38-39.

Howe, A. E. and Dreilinger, D. SavvySearch: a metasearch engine that learns which search engines to query. *AI Magazine*, 18, 1997, 19-25.

Hsu, C. and Ho, C. A hybrid case-based medical diagnosis system. In: *Proceedings of the Tenth IEEE International Conference on Tools with Artificial Intelligence*, pp. 359-366. Los Alamitos, CA, IEEE Computer Society, 1998.

Hu, C. An evaluation of a gateway system for automated online database selection. In: *Proceedings of the Ninth National Online Meeting*, pp. 107-114. Medford, NJ, Learned Information, 1988.

Hu, C. *An Evaluation of an Online Database Selection by a Gateway System with Artificial Intelligence Techniques*. Doctoral dissertation. Urbana-Champaign, University of Illinois, Graduate School of Library and Information Science, 1987.

Hui, S. C. and Goh, A. Incorporating abstract generation into an online retrieval interface for a library newspaper cutting system. *Aslib Proceedings*, 48, 1996, 259-265.

Humphrey, S. M. Interactive knowledge-based systems for improved subject analysis and retrieval. In: *Artificial Intelligence and Expert Systems: Will They Change the Library?*; ed. by F. W. Lancaster and L. C. Smith, pp. 81-117. Urbana-Champaign, University of Illinois, Graduate School of Library and Information Science, 1992.

Hunt, J. and Miles, R. Toward an intelligent architectural design aid. *Expert Systems*, 12(3), 1995, 209-218.

Huntington, D. Web-based AI: expert systems on the WWW. *PC AI*, 11(2), 1997, 20-23.

Hutchins, W. J. *Machine Translation: Past, Present, Future*. New York, Wiley, 1986.

Hutchins, W. J. and Somers, H. L. *An Introduction to Machine Translation*. New York, Academic Press, 1992.

Ibison, P. et al. Chemical literature data extraction: the CLIDE project. *Journal of Chemical Information and Computer Sciences*, 33, 1993, 338-344.

Indermaur, K. Baby steps. *Byte*, 20(3), 1995, 97-104.

Inoue, Y. Intelligent human resource management system: applications of expert system technology. *International Journal of Applied Expert Systems*, 1(3), 1993, 213-227.

Iyer, H. and Giguere, M. Towards designing an expert system to map mathematics classificatory structures. *Knowledge Organization*, 22, 1995, 141-147.

Jacob, V. S. and Bailey, A. D., Jr. A conceptual framework for the network approach to expert systems development in auditing. *Information Processing & Management*, 27, 1991, 481-497.

Jacobs, P. S. Introduction: text power and intelligent systems. In: *Text-Based Intelligent Systems*; ed. by P. S. Jacobs, pp. 1-8. Hillsdale, NJ, Lawrence Erlbaum, 1992a.

Jacobs, P. S. Joining statistics with NLP for text categorization. In: *Proceedings of the Third Conference on Applied Natural Language Processing*, pp. 178-185. San Francisco, CA, Morgan Kaufmann, 1992b.

Jacobs, P. S. Text-based systems and information management: artificial intelligence confronts matters of scale. *Proceedings* (of the) *6th International Conference on Tools with Artificial Intelligence*, pp. 235-236. Los Alamitos, CA, IEEE Computer Society Press, 1994.

Jacobs, P. S., ed. *Text-Based Intelligent Systems: Current Research and Practice in Information Extraction and Retrieval*. Hillsdale, NJ, Lawrence Erlbaum, 1992c.

Jacobs, P. S. and Rau, L. F. Innovations in text interpretation. In: *Natural Language Processing*; ed. by F. C. N. Pereira and B. J. Grosz, pp. 143-191. Cambridge, MA, MIT Press, 1994.

Jagadish, H. V. Indexing for retrieval by similarity. In: *Multimedia Database Systems*; ed. by V. S. Subrahmanian and S. Jajodia, pp. 165-184. Berlin, Springer-Verlag, 1996.

Jameel, A. Experiments with various neural network architectures for handwritten character recognition. In: *Proceedings* (of the) *Sixth International Conference on Tools With Artificial Intelligence*, pp. 548-554. Los Alamitos, CA, IEEE Computer Society Press, 1994.

Järvelin, K. A blueprint of an intermediary system for numeric source databases. In: *Information*Knowledge*Evolution*; ed. by S. Koskiala and R. Launo, pp. 311-320. Amsterdam, North-Holland, 1989.

Jeng, L. H. A converging vision of cataloging in the electronic world. *Information Technology and Libraries*, 15, 1996, 222-230.

Jeng, L. H. Modeling cataloging expertise: a feasibility study. *Information Processing & Management*, 30, 1994, 119-129.

Jeng, L. H. The structure of a knowledge base for cataloging rules. *Information Processing & Management*, 27, 1991, 97-110.

Jeng, L. H. *The Title Page as the Source of Information for Bibliographic Description: the Analysis of its Visual and Linguistic Characteristics.* Doctoral dissertation. Austin, University of Texas, Graduate School of Library and Information Science, 1987.

Jeng, L. H. and Weiss, K. B. Modeling cataloging expertise: a feasibility study. *Information Processing & Management,* 30, 1994, 119-129.

Johannes, L. Meet the doctor: a computer that knows a few things. *Wall Street Journal* (Eastern edition), December 18, 1995, B1.

Johnson, K. et al. A history-taking system that uses continuous speech recognition. In: *Supporting Collaboration:* (Proceedings of the) *Sixteenth Annual Symposium on Computer Applications in Medical Care,* pp. 757-761. New York, McGraw Hill, 1993.

Jones, E. K. and Roydhouse, A. Intelligent retrieval of archived meteorological data. *IEEE Expert,* 10(6), 1995, 50-57.

Jones, G. et al. The Video Mail Retrieval project: experiences in retrieving spoken documents. In: *Intelligent Multimedia Information Retrieval;* ed. by M. T. Maybury, pp. 191-214. Menlo Park, CA, AAAI Press, 1997.

Jones, K. Linguistic searching versus relevance ranking: DR-LINK and Target. *Online and CD-ROM Review,* 23(2), 1999, 67-80.

Jones, K. P. and Bell, C. L. M. Artificial intelligence program for indexing automatically (AIPIA). In: *Online Information 92,* pp. 187-196. Oxford, Learned Information, 1992.

Jörgensen, C. and Jörgensen, P. Hyperref: an expert system for the reference desk. In: *IOLS '91: Proceedings of the Sixth Integrated Online Library Systems Meeting,* pp. 75-82. Medford, NJ, Learned Information, 1991.

Joy, D. A. The KNOWS system on the Internet and Web. In: *Proceedings of the First Annual Conference on Emerging Technologies and Applications in Communications,* pp. 134-137. Los Alamitos, CA, IEEE Computer Society Press, 1996.

Kai, K. et al. TV newspapers in ISDB: multimedia information broadcasting services. *IEEE Transactions on Broadcasting*, 42, 1996, 187-193.

Kang, H. and Choi, K. Two-level document ranking using mutual information in natural language information retrieval. *Information Processing & Management*, 33, 1997, 289-306.

Kantor, P. B. Information retrieval techniques. *Annual Review of Information Science and Technology*, 29, 1994, 53-90.

Kassirer, J. P. A report card on computer-assisted diagnosis—the grade: C. *New England Journal of Medicine*, 330, 1994, 1824-1825.

Kataoka, M. et al. Music information retrieval system using complex-valued recurrent neural networks. In: *Proceedings of the 1998 IEEE Conference on Systems, Man, and Cybernetics*, pp. 4290-4295. Los Alamitos, CA, IEEE Computer Society, 1998.

Katz, J. The rights of kids in the digital age. *Wired*, 4(7), 1996, 120-123, 166-170.

Kerpedjiev, S. M. Automatic generation of multimodal weather reports from datasets. In: *Proceedings of the Third Conference on Applied Natural Language Processing*, pp. 48-55. San Francisco, CA, Morgan Kaufmann, 1992.

Khan, I. and Card, H. C. Personal adaptive Web agent: a tool for information filtering. In: *Proceedings of CCECE '97. Canadian Conference on Electrical and Computer Engineering. Engineering Innovation: Voyage of Discovery*, pp. 305-308. New York, IEEE, 1997.

Khan, I. et al. Categorizing Web documents using competitive learning: an ingredient of a personal adaptive agent. In: *Proceedings of the 1997 IEEE Conference on Neural Networks*, pp. 96-99. New York, IEEE, 1997.

Killingsworth, B. L. and McLeod, M. E. Factors affecting the acceptance and feasibility of expert systems in business. In: *Emerging Information Technologies for Competitive Advantage and Economic Development*; ed. by M. Khosrowpour, pp. 141-145. Harrisburg, PA, Idea Group Publishing, 1992.

Kim, Y. B. et al. Agent-based broadcasting with video indexing. *IEEE Transactions on Broadcasting*, 42, 1996, 215-221.

Kimmel, S. Robot-generated databases on the World Wide Web. *Database*, 19(1), 1996, 41-43, 46-49.

King, M. and McAulay, L. Barriers to adopting management expert systems: case studies of management accounting applications which failed. *Expert Systems*, 8, 1991, 139-147.

Korfhage, R. R. *Information Storage and Retrieval*. New York, Wiley, 1997.

Kranakis, E. et al. The complexity of data mining on the Web. In: *Proceedings of the Fifteenth Annual ACM Symposium on Principles of Distributed Computing*, p. 153. New York, Association for Computing Machinery, 1996.

Krulwich, B. and Burkey, C. The InfoFinder agent: learning user interests through heuristic phrase extraction. *IEEE Expert*, 12(5), 1997, 22-27.

Kukich, K. Spelling correction for the Telecommunications Network for the Deaf. *Communications of the ACM*, 35 (5), 1992, 80-90.

Kurita, T. and Kato, T. Learning of personal visual impressions for image database systems. In: *Proceedings of the Second International Conference on Document Analysis and Recognition*, pp. 547-552. Los Alamitos, CA, IEEE Computer Society Press, 1993.

Kurzke, C. et al. WebAssist: a user profile specific information retrieval assistant. *Computer Networks and ISDN Systems*, 30, 1998, 654-655.

LaGuardia, C. *Desk Set* revisited: reference librarians, reality, & research systems' design. *Journal of Academic Librarianship*, 21, 1995, 7-9.

Lambert, C. DIALOG Business Connection: the end-user solution? *Online Information 89*, pp. 161-168. Medford, NJ, Learned Information, 1989.

Lancaster, F. W. *Evaluation of the MEDLARS Demand Search Service.* Bethesda, MD, National Library of Medicine, 1968a.

Lancaster, F. W. *Indexing and Abstracting in Theory and Practice.* Second edition. Urbana-Champaign, University of Illinois, Graduate School of Library and Information Science, 1998.

Lancaster, F. W. *Information Retrieval Systems: Characteristics, Testing and Evaluation.* New York, Wiley, 1968b.

Lancaster, F. W. and Loescher, J. The corporate library and issues management. *Library Trends,* 43, 1994, 159-169.

Lancaster, F. W. and Neway, J. M. The future of indexing and abstracting services. *Journal of the American Society for Information Science,* 33, 1982, 183-189.

Langley, P. and Simon, H. A. Applications of machine learning and rule induction. *Communications of the ACM,* 38(11), 1995, 55-64.

Lanza, S. R. A cure for Web translation blues: Globalink. *Database,* 21(5), 1998, 57-59.

Laribi, A. and Laribi, S. A. An intelligent system to facilitate the diagnosis of adverse drug reactions. In: *Proceedings* (of the) *Sixth International Conference on Tools With Artificial Intelligence,* pp. 661-666. Los Alamitos, CA, IEEE Computer Society Press, 1994.

Larson, R. R. Experiments in automatic Library of Congress classification. *Journal of the American Society for Information Science,* 43, 1992, 130-148.

Law, D. Y. et al. An integrated case-based reasoning approach for intelligent help desk fault management. *Expert Systems with Applications,* 13, 1997, 265-274.

Lawson, M. et al. Automatic extraction of citations from the text of English-language patents—an example of template mining. *Journal of Information Science,* 22, 1996, 423-436.

Lee, Y. and Evens, M. W. Natural language interface for an expert system. *Expert Systems,* 15, 1998, 233-239.

Leinweber, D. J. and Beinart, Y. A little artificial intelligence goes a long way on Wall Street. *Journal of Portfolio Management,* 22, 1996, 95-106.

Levinson, S. E. Speech recognition technology: a critique. *Proceedings of the National Academy of Sciences,* 92, 1995, 9953-9955.

Lewin, H. C. HF-Explain: a natural language generation system for explaining a medical expert system. In: (Proceedings of the) *Fifteenth Annual Symposium on Computer Applications in Medical Care,* pp. 644-648. New York, McGraw Hill, 1992.

Liddy, E. D. Natural language processing for information retrieval and knowledge discovery. In: *Visualizing Subject Access for 21st Century Information Resources: Papers Presented at the 1997 Clinic on Library Applications of Data Processing,* pp. 137-147. Urbana-Champaign, University of Illinois, Graduate School of Library and Information Science, 1998.

Lienhart, R. et al. Video abstracting. *Communications of the ACM,* 40 (12), 1997, 54-62.

Lin, C. Y. Information access across the language barrier: the MuST system. In: *Proceedings of the 22nd Annual International Conference on Research and Development in Information Retrieval,* p. 330. New York, ACM, 1999.

Lin, X. Map displays for information retrieval. *Journal of the American Society for Information Science,* 48, 1997, 40-54.

Linthicum, D. S. Make voice response sing. *Byte,* 21(5), 1996, 53-54, 56.

Lirov, Y. and Lirov, V. Online search + logic programming = subject bibliography: an expert systems approach to bibliographic processing. *Online Review,* 14(1), 1990, 3-12.

Lu, C. et al. TheSys—a comprehensive thesaurus system for intelligent document analysis and text retrieval. In: *Proceedings of the Third International Conference on Document Analysis and Recognition.* Volume 2, pp. 1169-1173. Los Alamitos, CA, IEEE Computer Society Press, 1995.

Lucas, H. C., Jr. Market expert surveillance system. *Communications of the ACM*, 36(12), 1993, 27-34.

Maarek, Y. S. Automatically constructing simple help systems from natural language documentation. In: *Text-Based Intelligent Systems*; ed. by P. S. Jacobs, pp. 243-256. Hillsdale, NJ, Lawrence Erlbaum, 1992.

Maes, P. Agents that reduce work and information overload. *Communications of the ACM*, 37(7), 1994, 31-40, 146.

Magedanz, T. et al. Intelligent agents: an emerging technology for next generation telecommunications? In: *Proceedings of IEEE Infocom '96*. Volume 2, pp. 464-472. Los Alamitos, CA, IEEE Computer Society Press, 1996.

Mahadevan, S. et al. An apprentice-based approach to knowledge acquisition. *Artificial Intelligence*, 64 (1), 1993, 1-52.

Main, A. and Weckert, J. In defence of simple expert systems: a case study with some observations. *LASIE*, 23 (4/5), 1993, 62-70.

Mallen, E. Intelligent character recognition: it's not just recognition anymore. *Bulletin of the American Society for Information Science*, 18(5), 1992, 9-11.

Mani, I. et al. Towards content-based browsing of broadcast news video. In: *Intelligent Multimedia Information Retrieval*; ed. by M. T. Maybury, pp. 241-258. Menlo Park, CA, AAAI Press, 1997.

Markowitz, J. A. *Using Speech Recognition*. Upper Saddle River, NJ, Prentice Hall PTR, 1996.

Markus, M. L. and Keil, M. If we build it, they will come: designing information systems that people want to use. *Sloan Management Review*, 35(4), 1994, 11-25.

Martin, P. et al. SpeechActs: a spoken-language framework. *Computer*, 29, July 1996, 33-40.

Martin-Bautista, M. J. A fuzzy genetic algorithm approach to an adaptive information retrieval agent. *Journal of the American Society for Information Science*, 50, 1999, 760-771.

Martinez, C. et al. An expert system for machine-aided indexing. *Journal of Chemical Information and Computer Sciences*, 27, 1987, 158-162.

Mason, P. R. and Sample, T. A. Knowledge engineering for home landscaping: the Plant Expert Advisor. In: *Information Technology: IT's for Everyone*; ed. by T. W. Leonhardt, pp. 84-86. Chicago, IL, American Library Association, 1992.

Matsumoto, K. An experimental agricultural data mining system. In: *Proceedings of the First International Conference on Discovery Science*, pp. 439-440. Berlin, Springer-Verlag, 1998.

Maybury, M. T. Generating summaries from event data. *Information Processing & Management*, 31, 1995, 735-751.

McCarthy, M. V. InfoMaster: a powerful information retrieval service for business. *Online*, 10 (6), 1986, 53-58.

McCleary, H. Filtered information services. *Online*, 18(4), 1994, 33-42.

McDonald, D. D. Robust partial-parsing through incremental, multi-algorithm processing. In: *Text-Based Intelligent Systems*; ed. by P. S. Jacobs, pp. 83-99. Hillsdale, NJ, Lawrence Erlbaum, 1992.

McKenna, B. Humanware? *Online and CD-ROM Review*, 23 (1), 1999, 43-47.

McKeown, K. et al. Generating concise natural language summaries. *Information Processing & Management*, 31, 1995, 703-733.

McKiernan, G. ABCD: agent-based collection development with intelligent agent software at Iowa State University. *Technicalities*, 18(9), 1998, 8-10.

Meador, J. M., Jr. and Cline, L. Displaying and utilizing selection tools in a user-friendly electronic environment. *Library Acquisitions: Practice & Theory*, 16, 1992, 289-294.

Meador, R. III and Wittig, G. R. AACR2 rules used in assigning access points for books in two subjects: implications for automatic cataloging expert systems. *Library Resources & Technical Services*, 35, 1991, 135-140.

Mehrotra, R. and Gary, J. E. Similar-shape retrieval in shape data management. *Computer*, 28(9), 1995, 57-62.

Mehtre, B. M. et al. Shape measures for content based image retrieval: a comparison. *Information Processing & Management*, 33, 1997, 319-337.

Mellisch, C. and Dale, R. Evaluation in the context of natural language generation. *Computer Speech and Language*, 12, 1998, 349-373.

Mena, J. Automatic data mining. *PC AI*, 10 (6), 1996, 16-18. 20.

Mendes, M. et al. Agents skills and their roles in mobile computing and personal communications. In: (Proceedings of the) *IFIP World Conference on Mobile Communications*, pp. 181-204. New York, Chapman & Hall, 1996.

Metzger, P. ANYTHING GOES! An expert system for information sources in American musical theater. *Library Software Review*, 12, Summer 1993, 23-31.

Meyer, D. E. and Ruiz, D. End-user selection of databases. *Database*, 13 (3), 1990, 21-29; 13 (4), 1990, 35-42; 13 (5), 1990, 59-67.

Miller, G. A. WordNet: a lexical database for English. *Communications of the ACM*, 38(11), 1995, 39-41.

Milosavljevic, M. and Oberlander, J. Dynamic catalogues on the WWW. *Computer Networks and ISDN Systems*, 30, 1998, 666-668.

Mitchell, T. et al. Experience with a learning personal assistant. *Communications of the ACM*, 37(7), 1994, 81-91.

Molto, M. and Svenonius, E. Automatic recognition of title page names. *Information Processing & Management*, 27, 1991, 83-95.

Morgan, E. L. Clarence meets Alcuin: expert systems are still an option in reference work. In: *The Cybrarian's Manual*, pp. 127-134. Chicago, American Library Association, 1997.

Morris, A. Online company database selection: an evaluation of directories and CIDA (an expert system). *Journal of Information Science*, 20, 1994, 260-269.

Morris, A. Personal communication, October 1996.

Morris, A. et al. CIDA: the expert Company Information Database Adviser. *Journal of Information Science*, 20, 1994, 247-259.

Morris, A. et al. MOSS: a prototype expert system for modifying online search strategies. In: *Online Information 89 Proceedings*, pp. 415-434. Oxford, Learned Information, 1989.

Morrisey, F. Using computer-based library reference guides: a comparison of hypertext programs with expert systems. *Library Hi Tech*, 10(1/2), 1992, 61-64.

Mostafa, J. et al. A multilevel approach to intelligent information filtering: model, system, and evaluation. *ACM Transactions on Information Systems*, 15, 1997, 368-399.

Moynihan, G. P. et al. An object-oriented system for ergonomic risk assessment. *Expert Systems*, 12(2), 1995, 149-156.

Murugesan, S. Intelligent agents on the Internet and Web. In: *Proceedings of the IEEE Region 10 Conference on Global Connectivitiy in Energy, Computer, Communication and Control (TENCON)*, pp. 97-102. Piscataway, NJ, IEEE, 1998.

Myers, B. et al. Strategic directions in human-computer interaction. *ACM Computing Surveys*, 28, 1996, 794-809.

Nakagawa, M. et al. Principles of pen interface design for creative work. In: *Proceedings of the Second International Conference on Document Analysis and Recognition*, pp. 718-721. Los Alamitos, CA, IEEE Computer Society Press, 1993.

Nakamura, Y. et al. Diagram understanding utilizing natural language text. In: *Proceedings of the Second International Conference on Document Analysis and Recognition*, pp. 614-618. Los Alamitos, CA, IEEE Computer Society Press, 1993.

Nardi, B. A. and O'Day, V. Applications and implications of agent technology for libraries. *Electronic Library*, 16, 1998, 325-337.

Nardi, B. A. and O'Day, V. Intelligent agents: what we learned at the library. *Libri*, 46, 1996, 59-88.

Nardi, B. A. et al. Collaborative, programmable intelligent agents. *Communications of the ACM*, 41(3), 1998, 96-104.

Nath, I. Machine translation—theories that make computers translate. *Information Studies*, 5, 1999, 7-24.

Ng, H. T. et al. Feature selection, perception learning, and a usability case study for text categorization. In: *SIGIR '97: Proceedings of the 20th Annual International ACM SIGIR Conference on Research and Development in Information Retrieval*, pp. 67-73. New York, Association for Computing Machinery, 1997.

Nicholson, S. Indexing and abstracting on the World Wide Web: an examination of six web databases. *Information Technology and Libraries*, 16, 1997, 73-81.

No more expert systems: the intelligent technology that got left behind. *Critical Technology Trends*, Report No. 3, March 1994.

Notess, G. R. Mega-searching from the desktop. *Online*, 21(3), 1997, 89-91.

Nunamaker, N. F. Future research in group support systems: needs, some questions and possible directions. *International Journal of Human-Computer Studies*, 47, 1997, 357-385.

Nye, J. B. Integrating serials into the Triangle Research Libraries Network Document Delivery System. *Serials Librarian*, 31(3), 1997, 29-48.

Oakman, R. L. The evolution of intelligent writing assistants: trends and future prospects. In: *Proceedings* (of the) *Sixth International Conference on Tools With Artificial Intelligence*, pp. 233-234. Los Alamitos, CA, IEEE Computer Society Press, 1994.

Obradovich, J. H. et al. The Transfusion Medicine Tutor: the use of expert-systems technology to teach students and provide support to practitioners in antibody identification. In: *Proceedings of the International Conference on the Learning Sciences, 1996*; ed. by D. C. Edelson and E. A. Domeshek, pp. 249-255. Charlottesville, VA, Association for the Advancement of Computing in Education, 1996.

Ogle, V. E. and Stonebraker, M. Chabot: retrieval from a relational database of images. *Computer*, 28(9), 1995, 40-48.

O'Leary, M. Easynet revisited: pushing the online frontier. *Online*, 12 (5), 1988, 22-30.

Oliver, D. E. and Altman, R. B. Extraction of SNOMED concepts from medical record texts. In: *Transforming Information, Changing Health Care: Proceedings* (of the) *Eighteenth Annual Symposium on Computer Applications in Medical Care*, pp. 179-183. Philadelphia, PA, Hanley & Belfus, 1994.

Oravec, J. A. and Travis, L. If we could do it over, we'd . . . learning from less-than-successful expert system projects. *Journal of Systems Software*, 19, 1992, 113-122.

Ordille, J. J. When agents roam, who can you trust? In: *Proceedings of the First Annual Conference on Emerging Technologies and Applications in Communications*, pp. 188-191. Los Alamitos, CA, IEEE Computer Society Press, 1996.

Ozaki, K. et al. Semantic retrieval on art museum database system. In: (Proceedings of the) *1996 IEEE International Conference on Systems, Man and Cybernetics*, pp. 2109-2112. Piscataway, NJ, Institute of Electrical and Electronics Engineers, 1996.

Paice, C. D. and Jones, P. A. The identification of important concepts in highly structured technical papers. In: *SIGIR '93: Proceedings of the Sixteenth Annual International ACM SIGIR Conference on Research and Development in Information Retrieval*, pp. 69-78. New York, Association for Computing Machinery, 1993.

Pandit, M. S. and Kalbag, S. The Selection Recognition Agent: instant access to relevant information and operations. *Knowledge-Based Systems*, 10, 1998, 304-310.

Patel, N. V. and Sethi, I. K. Audio characterization for video indexing. In: *Storage and Retrieval for Still Image and Video Databases IV*; ed. by I. K. Sethi and R. C. Jain, pp. 373-384. Bellingham, WA, International Society for Optical Engineering, 1996.

Patel, N. V. and Sethi, I. K. Video classification using speaker identification. In: *Storage and Retrieval for Image and Video Databases V*; ed. by I. K. Sethi and R. C. Jain, pp. 218-225. Bellingham, WA, International Society for Optical Engineering, 1997.

Pazzani, M. et al. Learning from hotlists and coldlists: towards a WWW information filtering and seeking agent. In: *Proceedings* (of the) *Seventh International Conference on Tools With Artificial Intelligence*, pp. 492-495. Los Alamitos, CA, IEEE Computer Society Press, 1995.

Pereira, F. C. N. and Grosz, B. J. *Natural Language Processing*. Cambridge, MA, MIT Press, 1994.

Perez-Carballo, J. and Strzalkowski, T. Natural language information retrieval: a progress report. *Information Processing & Management*, 36, 2000, 155-178.

Perkowitz, M. et al. Learning to understand information on the Internet: an example-based approach. *Journal of Intelligent Information Systems*, 8, 1997, 133-153.

Pfaffenberger, B. *Web Search Strategies*. New York, MIS Press, 1996.

Picard, R. W. A society of models for video and image libraries. *IBM Systems Journal*, 35, 1996, 292-312.

Picard, R. W. and Minka, T. P. Vision texture for annotation. *Multimedia Systems*, 3, 1995, 3-14.

Piraino, D. W. et al. Problems in applying expert system technology to radiographic image interpretation. *Journal of Digital Imaging*, 2(1), 1989, 21-26.

Pollitt, A. S. Intelligent interfaces to online databases. *Expert Systems for Information Management*, 3(1), 1990, 49-69.

Pontigo, J. et al. Expert systems in document delivery: the feasibility of learning capabilities. In: *Artificial Intelligence and Expert Systems: Will They Change the Library?*; ed. by F. W. Lancaster and L. C. Smith, pp. 254-266. Urbana-Champaign, University of Illinois, Graduate School of Library and Information Science, 1992.

Poo, D. C. et al. Design and implementation of the E-Referencer. *Data & Knowledge Engineering*, 32, 2000, 199-218.

Poon, A. D. and Fagan, L. M. PEN-Ivory: the design and evaluation of a pen-based computer system for structured data entry. In: *Transforming Information, Changing Health Care: Proceedings* (of the) *Eighteenth Annual Symposium on Computer Applications in Medical Care*, pp. 447-451. Philadelphia, PA, Hanley & Belfus, 1994.

Poulter, A. et al. LIS professionals as knowledge engineers. *Annual Review of Information Science and Technology*, 29, 1994, 305-350.

Pozzi, S. and Celentano, A. Knowledge-based document filing. *IEEE Expert*, 8(5), 1993, 34-45.

Prabha, C. The large retrieval phenomenon. *Advances in Library Automation and Networking*, 4, 1991, 55-92.

Pritchard-Schoch, T. Natural language comes of age. *Online*, 17(3), 1993, 33-43.

Proceedings of the Third International Conference on Document Analysis and Recognition. 2 volumes. Los Alamitos, CA, IEEE Computer Society Press, 1995.

Proper, H. A. and Bruza, P. D. What is information discovery about? *Journal of the American Society for Information Science*, 50, 1999, 737-750.

Qin, J. and Norton, M. J., eds. Knowledge discovery in bibliographic databases. *Library Trends*, 48(1), Summer 1999 (complete issue).

Quantrille, T. E. and Liu, Y. A. *Artificial Intelligence in Chemical Engineering*. San Diego, CA, Academic Press, 1991.

Quintana, Y. Knowledge-based information filtering of financial information. In: *Proceedings of the 1997 National Online Meeting*, pp. 279-285. Medford, NJ, Information Today, 1997.

Rada, R. et al. Computerized guides to journal selection. *Information Technology and Libraries*, 6, 1987, 173-184.

Raggad, B. C. Expert system quality control. *Information Processing & Management*, 32, 1996, 171-183.

Ragusa, J. M. and Turban, E. Integrating expert systems and multimedia: a review of the literature. *International Journal of Applied Expert Systems*, 2(1), 1994, 54-71.

Raitt, D. The library of the future. In: *Libraries and the Future: Essays on the Library in the Twenty-first Century*; ed. by F. W. Lancaster, pp. 61-72. New York, Haworth Press, 1993.

Rajagopalan, R. The Figure Understander: a tool for the integration of text and graphical input to a knowledge base. In: *Proceedings* (of the) *Sixth International Conference on Tools With Artificial Intelligence*, pp. 80-87. Los Alamitos, CA, IEEE Computer Society Press, 1994.

Rapaport, J. Intelligent business applications: target marketing. *PC AI*, 9(6), 1995, 20-22.

Rapaport, J. Intelligent business applications: customer service. *PC AI*, 10(2), 1996, 34-37.

Rapoza, J. Service filters news for intranets. *PC Week*, 13(21), 1996a, N_1, N_7, N_{12}.

Rapoza, J. A smart way to put help on the Web. *PC Week*, 13(39), 1996b, 93.

Rasmus, D.W. Groupware: reconnecting with human intelligence. *PC AI*, 9(6), 1995, 27-28, 30, 32-34.

Rasmus, D. W. Mind tools: connecting to groupware. *PC AI*, 10(5), 1996, 32-36.

Rasmus, D. W. The object of workflow. *PC AI*, 11(2), 1997, 16-19.

Rasmussen, E. M. Indexing images. *Annual Review of Information Science and Technology*, 32, 1997, 167-196.

Reategui, E. B. et al. Combining a neural network with case-based reasoning in a diagnostic system. *Artificial Intelligence in Medicine*, 9, 1997, 5-27.

Resnick, P. and Varian, H. R., eds. Recommender systems. *Communications of the ACM*, 40(3), 1997, 56-89.

Richardson, E. C. Add an engine. *Internet World*, 7(5), 1996, 88, 90, 92.

Richardson, J. V., Jr. and Reyes, R. B. Government information expert systems: a quantitative evaluation. *College & Research Libraries*, 56, 1995, 235-247.

Riedel, W. R. Personal communication, November 1996.

Riloff, E. and Lehnert, W. Automated dictionary construction for information extraction from text. In: (Proceedings of the) *Ninth Conference on Artificial Intelligence for Applications*, pp. 93-99. Los Alamitos, CA, IEEE Computer Society Press, 1993.

Roberts, L. K. Evaluation of the Easynet gateway. In: *Proceedings of the Seventh National Online Meeting*, pp. 375-381. Medford, NJ, Learned Information, 1986.

Roesler, M. and Hawkins, D. T. Intelligent agents. *Online*, 18(4), 1994, 19-32.

Rowe, N. C. Inferring depictions in natural-language captions for efficient access to picture data. *Information Processing & Management*, 30, 1994, 379-388.

Rowe, N. C. Precise and efficient access to captioned picture libraries: the MARIE Project. *Library Trends*, 48, 1999, 475-495.

Rowe, N. C. and Frew, B. *Automatic Caption Localization for Photographs on World Wide Web Pages.* Monterey, CA, Naval Postgraduate School, Computer Science Department, 1996.

Rowe, N. C. and Frew, B. Automatic classification of objects in captioned depictive photographs for retrieval. In: *Intelligent Multimedia Information Retrieval*; ed. by M. Maybury, pp. 65-79. Palo Alto, CA, AAAI Press, 1997.

Rowe, N. C. and Guglielmo, E. J. Exploiting captions in retrieval of multimedia data. *Information Processing & Management*, 29, 1993, 453-461.

Rudnicky, A. I. et al. Survey of current speech technology. *Communications of the ACM*, 37(3), 1994, 52-57.

Rui, Y. et al. Information retrieval beyond the text document. *Library Trends*, 48, 1999, 455-474.

Rumelhart, D. E. et al. The basic ideas in neural networks. *Communications of the ACM*, 37(3), 1994, 87-92.

Saarenvirta, G. Data mining to improve profitability. *CMA Magazine*, 72 (2), 1998, 8-12.

Salamon, R. Expert systems in medicine. *World Health*, August/September 1989, 12-13.

Salton, G. Expert systems and information retrieval. *SIGIR Forum*, 31(1), 1997, 39-42.

Salton, G. and Buckley, C. Automatic text structuring experiments. In: *Text-Based Intelligent Systems*; ed. by P. S. Jacobs, pp. 199-210. Hillsdale, NJ, Lawrence Erlbaum, 1992.

Salton, G. and McGill, M. J. *Introduction to Modern Information Retrieval.* New York, McGraw-Hill, 1983.

Sandberg-Fox, A. M. *The Amenability of a Cataloging Process to Simulation by Automatic Techniques.* Doctoral dissertation. Urbana-Champaign, University of Illinois, Graduate School of Library Science, 1972. (ED 076225)

Sandberg-Fox, A. M. Selection of main entry: a conceptual model. In: *Expert Systems in Libraries*; ed. by R. Aluri and D. E. Riggs, pp. 135-154. Norwood, NJ, Ablex Publishing, 1990.

Sauperl, A. and Saye, J. D. Pebbles for the mosaic of cataloging expertise: what do problems in expert systems for cataloging reveal about cataloging expertise? *Library Resources and Technical Services*, 43, 1999, 78-94.

Savić, D. Automatic classification of office documents: review of available methods and techniques. *Records Management Quarterly*, 29(4), 1995, 3-6, 8-18.

Scales, B. J. and Felt, E. C. Diversity on the World Wide Web: using robots to search the Web. *Library Software Review*, 14, 1995, 132-136.

Schatz, B. et al. Federating diverse collections of scientific literature. *Computer*, 29(5), 1996, 28-36.

Schmidt, J. and Putz, W. Knowledge acquisition and representation for document structure recognition: the CAROL project. In: *Proceedings of the Ninth Conference on Artificial Intelligence for Applications*, pp. 177-181. Los Alamitos, CA, IEEE Computer Society Press, 1993.

Schmuller, J. The bottom of the tenth. *PC AI*, 10 (6), 1996, 8.

Schultz, L. Designing an expert system to assign Dewey classification numbers to scores. *Proceedings of the Tenth National Online Meeting*, pp. 393-397. Medford, NJ, Learned Information, 1989.

Seachrist, D. Help-desk helpers. *Byte*, 21(5), 1996, 138-141.

Sears, D. S. Computer Assisted Practice System (CAPS) and its application in support of the reference function within the law library. *Legal Reference Services Quarterly*, 13(4), 1994, 5-18.

Selker, T. COACH: a teaching agent that learns. *Communications of the ACM*, 37(7), 1994, 92-99.

Semeraro, G. et al. Learning contextual rules for document under-standing. In: *Proceedings* (of the) *Tenth Conference on Artificial Intelligence for Applications*, pp. 108-115. Los Alamitos, CA, IEEE Computer Society Press, 1994.

Shao, Y. P. et al. Expert systems in UK banking. In: *Proceedings* (of) *the 11th Conference on Artificial Intelligence for Applications*, pp. 18-23. Los Alamitos, CA, IEEE Computer Society Press, 1995.

Shapira, B. et al. Stereotypes in information filtering systems. *Information Processing & Management*, 33, 1997, 273-287.

Sharma, R. et al. A framework for the design and implementation of groupware. In: (Proceedings of the) *1994 IEEE International Conference on Systems, Man, and Cybernetics*, pp. 1891-1897. New York, Institute of Electrical and Electronics Engineers, 1994.

Shepherd, A. Knowledge-based systems: critiquing versus conven-tional approaches. *Expert Systems with Applications*, 14, 1998, 433-441.

Shiffman, S. et al. The integration of a continuous-speech-recogni-tion system with the QMR diagnostic program. In: *Supporting Collaboration:* (Proceedings of the) *Sixteenth Annual Symposium on Computer Applications in Medical Care*, pp. 767-771. New York, McGraw Hill, 1993.

Shute, S. J. and Smith, P. J. Knowledge-based search tactics. *Information Processing & Management*, 29, 1993, 29-45.

Silverman, B. G. Survey of expert critiquing systems: practical and theoretical frontiers. *Communications of the ACM*, 35(4), 1992, 106-127.

Silvester, J. P. et al. *Machine Aided Indexing from Natural Language Text. Status Report.* Linthicum Heights, MD, RMS Associates, 1993. NASA-CR-4512.

Simon, H. A. Artificial intelligence: an empirical science. *Artificial Intelligence*, 77, 1995, 95-127.

Singhal, A. and Pereira, F. Document expansion for speech retrieval. In: *SIGIR '99: Proceedings of the 22nd Annual International ACM SIGIR Conference on Research and Development in Information Retrieval*, pp. 34-41. New York, Association for Computing Machiney, 1999.

Smeaton, A. F. and Harman, D. The TREC experiments and their impact on Europe. *Journal of Information Science*, 23, 1997, 169-174.

Smith, A. G. Expert systems in reference work: robot at the reference desk or electronic Walford? In: *Libraries: the Heart of the Matter*, pp. 337-340. Deakin, ACT, Australian Library and Information Association, 1992.

Smith, A. G. Kiwinet Advisor: a knowledge base for the selection of online databases. *LASIE*, 22 (1), 1991, 4-17.

Smith, A. G. Personal communication, November 1996.

Smith, D. et al. *Using the New AACR2: an Expert Systems Approach to Choice of Access Points*. London, Library Association, 1993.

Smith, F. J. et al. Voice access to BLAISE. In: *Online Information 89*, pp. 1-12. Oxford, Learned Information, 1989.

Smith, G. L. Generation of electronic product documentation. In: *Innovative Applications of Artificial Intelligence 2*; ed. by A. Rappaport and R. Smith, pp. 189-200. Cambridge, MA, MIT Press, 1991.

Smith, J. R. and Chang, S. F. An image and video search engine for the World-Wide Web. In: *Storage and Retrieval for Image and Video Databases V*; ed. by I. K. Sethi and R. C. Jain, pp. 84-95. Bellingham, WA, International Society for Optical Engineering, 1997a.

Smith, J. R. and Chang, S. F. Querying by color regions using the VisualSEEK content-based visual query system. In: *Intelligent Multimedia Information Retrieval*; ed. by M. T. Maybury, pp. 23-41. Menlo Park, CA, AAAI Press, 1997b.

Smith, K. F. Personal communication, November 1996.

Smith, K. F. POINTER: the microcomputer reference program for federal documents. In: *Expert Systems in Libraries*; ed. by R. Aluri and D. E. Riggs, pp. 41-50. Norwood, NJ, Ablex Publishing, 1990.

Smith, M. H. et al. Fuzzy data mining for querying and retrieval of research archival information. In: *1998 Conference of the North American Fuzzy Information Processing Society (NAFIP)*, pp. 140-145. New York, IEEE, 1998.

Sowell, S. L. Expanding horizons in collection development with expert systems: development and testing of a demonstration prototype. *Special Libraries*, 80, 1989, 45-50.

Sparck Jones, K. Further reflections on TREC. *Information Processing & Managment*, 36, 2000, 37-85.

Sparck Jones, K. Personal communication. February 13, 1997.

Sparck Jones, K. Reflections on TREC. *Information Processing & Management*, 31(3), 1995, 291-314.

Sparck Jones, K. The role of artificial intelligence in information retrieval. *Journal of the American Society for Information Science*, 42, 1991, 558-565.

Sparck Jones, K. et al. Experiments in spoken document retrieval. *Information Processing & Management*, 32, 1996, 399-417.

Spink, A. and Losee, R. M. Feedback in information retrieval. *Annual Review of Information Science and Technology*, 31, 1996, 33-78.

Springer, S. et al. Automatic letter composition for customer service. In: *Innovative Applications of Artificial Intelligence 3*; ed. by R. G. Smith and A. C. Scott, pp. 67-83. Menlo Park, CA, AAAI Press, 1991.

Srihari, R. K. Automatic indexing and content-based retrieval of captioned photographs. In: *Proceedings of the Third International Conference on Document Analysis and Recognition*. Volume 2, pp. 1165-1168. Los Alamitos, CA, IEEE Computer Society Press, 1995.

Srihari, R. K. Intelligent document understanding: understanding photographs with captions. In: *Proceedings of the Second International Conference on Document Analysis and Recognition*, pp. 664-667. Los Alamitos, CA, IEEE Computer Society Press, 1993.

Srihari, R. K. and Zhang, Z. Exploiting multimodal context in image retrieval. *Library Trends*, 48, 1999, 496-520.

St. Clair, D. C. et al. Intelligent search engine for finding graphics objects. In: *Proceedings of the 1998 Artificial Networks in Engineering Conference*, pp. 425-430. Fairfield, NJ, ASME, 1998.

Stanfill, C. and Waltz, D. L. Statistical methods, artificial intelligence, and information retrieval. In: *Text-Based Intelligent Systems*; ed. by P. S. Jacobs, pp. 215-225. Hillsdale, NJ, Lawrence Erlbaum, 1992.

Stern, D. From the all-in-one workstation to seamless networks: a strategic plan. *Online*, 21(2), 1997, 46-55.

Stock, O. ALFRESCO: enjoying the combination of natural language processing and hypermedia for information exploration. In: *Intelligent Multimedia Interfaces*; ed. by M. T. Maybury, pp. 197-224. Cambridge, MA, MIT Press, 1993.

Su, S. F. and Lancaster, F. W. Evaluation of expert systems in reference service applications. *RQ*, 35, 1995, 219-228.

Sundheim, B. M. Overview of results of the MUC-6 evaluation. In: *Proceedings of the Sixth Message Understanding Conference (MUC-6)*, pp. 13-31. San Francisco, CA, Morgan Kaufmann, 1995.

Sussman, S. and Ng, F. Business travel counseling. *Annals of Tourism Research*, 22, 1995, 688-690.

Svenonius, E. and Molto, M. Automatic derivation of name access points in cataloging. *Journal of the American Society for Information Science*, 41, 1990, 254-263.

Swaby, P. A. Integrating artificial intelligence and graphics in a tool for microfossil identification for use in the petroleum industry. In: *Innovative Applications of Artificial Intelligence 2*; ed. by A. Rappaport and R. Smith, pp. 203-218. Cambridge, MA, MIT Press, 1991.

Swanson, D. R. Intervening in the life cycles of scientific knowledge. *Library Trends*, 41, 1993, 606-631.

Syiam, M. M. A neural network expert system for diagnosing eye diseases. In: *Proceedings* (of the) *Tenth Conference on Artificial Intelligence for Applications*, pp. 491-492. Los Alamitos, CA, IEEE Computer Society Press, 1994.

Taussig, K. and Bernstein, J. Macrophone: an American English telephone speech corpus. In: *Human Language Technology: Proceedings of a Workshop held at Plainsboro, New Jersey, March 8-11, 1994*, pp. 27-30. San Francisco, CA, Morgan Kaufmann, 1994.

Tegenbos, J. and Nieuwenhuysen, P. My kingdom for an agent? Evaluation of Autonomy, an intelligent search agent for the Internet. *Online and CD-ROM Review*, 21, 1997, 139-148.

Tenopir, C. Front-end software proliferates. *Library Journal*, 121(8), 1996, 29-30.

Thé, L. Morph your help desk into customer support. *Datamation*, 42, January 15, 1996, 52-54.

Thomas, C. G. BASAR: a framework for integrating agents in the World Wide Web. *Computer*, 28, May 1995, 84-86.

Thomas, K. Personal communication, November 1996.

Thomas K. and Hadgraft, R. The information superhighway and teaching information searching skills to engineers. In: *Proceedings of the 3rd East-West Congress on Engineering Education*, pp. 417-421, 1996. Melbourne, International Centre for Engineering Education, 1996.

Thompson, R. et al. Evaluating Dewey concepts as a knowledge base for automatic subject assignment. http://orc.rsch.oclc.org:6109/eval_dc.html February 12, 1997.

Thornburg, G. E. *LOOK: Implementation of an Expert System in Information Retrieval for Database Selection*. Doctoral dissertation. Urbana-Champaign, University of Illinois, Graduate School of Library and Information Science, 1987.

Thurman, D. A. et al. Design of an intelligent Web-based help desk system. In: *1997 IEEE International Conference on Systems, Man, and Cybernetics. Computational Cybernetics and Simulation*, pp. 2198-2203. New York, IEEE, 1997.

Tilson, Y. and East, H. Academic scientists' reaction to end-user services: observations on a trial service giving access to Medline using the Grateful Med software. *Online & CDROM Review*, 18, 1994, 71-77.

Trautman, R. and Flittner, S. von. An expert system for microcomputers to aid selection of online databases. *Reference Librarian*, 23, 1989, 207-238.

Trybula, W. J. Data mining and knowledge discovery. In: *Annual Review of Information Science and Technology*, pp. 197-229. Medford, NJ, Information Today, 1997.

Tseng, G. Expert systems and online information retrieval. In: *The Application of Expert Systems in Libraries and Information Centres*; ed. by A. Morris, pp. 167-193. London, Bowker-Saur, 1992.

Tseng, G. et al. Expert selection of databases for UK company news. In: *Online Information 94*, pp. 75-85. Medford, NJ, Learned Information, 1994.

Tseng, G. et al. The selection of online databases for UK company information. *Journal of Librarianship and Information Science*, 27, 1995, 159-170.

Tway, L. E. and Riedel, W. R. Intelligent data entry. *PC AI*, 10 (1), 1996, 16-21.

Uthurusamy, R. et al. Extracting knowledge from diagnostic databases. *IEEE Expert*, 8(6), 1993, 27-38.

van Brakel, P. A. EasyNet: intelligent gateway to online searching. *South African Journal of Library and Information Science*, 56, 1988, 191-197.

Van Dyne, M. M. et al. Using machine learning and expert systems to predict preterm delivery in pregnant women. In: *Proceedings* (of the) *Tenth Conference on Artificial Intelligence for Applications*, pp. 344-350. Los Alamitos, CA, IEEE Computer Society Press, 1994.

Varney, S. Link your help desk to the Web. *Datamation*, 42 (10), 1996, 64-67.

Vedder, R. G. et al. Five PC-based expert systems for business reference: an evaluation. *Information Technology and Libraries*, 8, 1989, 42-54.

Venditto, G. Search engine showdown. *Internet World*, 7(5), 1996, 79-86.

Verity, J. W. Coaxing meaning out of raw data. *Business Week*, February 3, 1997, 134-138.

Vickery, B. C. Intelligent interfaces to online databases. In: *Artificial Intelligence and Expert Systems: Will They Change the Library?*; ed. by F. W. Lancaster and L. C. Smith, pp. 239-253. Urbana, IL, Graduate School of Library and Information Science, University of Illinois, 1992.

Vickery, B. C. Knowledge discovery from databases: an introductory review. *Journal of Documentation*, 53, 1997, 107-122.

Vickery, B. C. and Vickery, A. An application of language processing for a search interface. *Journal of Documentation*, 48, 1992, 255-275.

Vít, C. et al. Information system for onco-pathology: from an expert system to WWW. In: *Database and Expert Systems Applications*; ed. by N. Revell and A Min Tjoa, pp. 642-651. Berlin, Springer-Verlag, 1995. (Lecture Notes in Computer Science, Volume 978)

Vizine-Goetz, D. OCLC investigates using classification tools to organize Internet data. In: *Visualizing Subject Access for 21st Century Information Resources: Papers Presented at the 1997 Clinic on Library Applications of Data Processing*, pp. 93-105. Urbana-Champaign, University of Illinois, Graduate School of Library and Information Science, 1998.

Vizine-Goetz, D. et al. Automating descriptive cataloging. In: *Expert Systems in Libraries*; ed. by R. Aluri and D. E. Riggs, pp. 123-134. Norwood, NJ, Ablex Publishing, 1990.

von Wahlde, B. and Schiller, N. Creating the virtual library: strategic issues. In: *The Virtual Library: Visions and Realities*; ed. by L. M. Saunders, pp. 15-46. Westport, CT, Meckler, 1993.

Voorhees, E. M. and Harman, D. Overview of the sixth Text Retrieval Conference (TREC-6). *Information Processing & Management*, 36, 2000, 3-35.

Voorhees, E. M. and Kantor, P. TREC-5 confusion track. Contribution to the Text Retrieval Conference (TREC-5), November 20-22, 1996.

Wactlar, H. D. et al. Lessons learned from building a terabyte digital video library. *Computer*, 32(2), 1999, 66-73.

Waldstein, R. K. Library—an electronic ordering system. *Information Processing & Management*, 22, 1986, 39-44.

Walker, N. and Truman, G. Neural networks for data mining electronic text collections. In: *Proceedings of the SPIE—The International Society for Optical Engineering Conference*, pp. 299-306. Bellingham, WA, SPIE, 1997.

Walsh, J. Intel LANDesk lets users cry for help from Web browsers. *InfoWorld*, 18(39), 1996, 12.

Walter, V. A. Becoming digital: policy implications for library youth services. *Library Trends*, 45, 1997, 585-601.

Warner, E. Expert systems and the law. *High Technology Business*, 8(10), 1988, 32-35.

Waters, S. T. Expert systems at the National Agricultural Library: past, present, and future. In: *Artificial Intelligence and Expert Systems: Will They Change the Library?*; ed. by F. W. Lancaster and L. C. Smith, pp. 161-177. Urbana-Champaign, University of Illinois, Graduate School of Library and Information Science, 1992.

Watson, J. et al. Internet text retrieval: benchmark study. *Inform*, 10(4), 1996, 24-45.

Watters, P. A. and Patel, M. Semantic processing performance of Internet machine translation systems. *Internet Research*, 9, 1999, 153-160.

Watterson, K. A data miner's tools. *Byte*, 20, October 1995, 91-92, 94, 96.

Weckert, J. How expert can expert systems really be? In: *Libraries and Expert Systems*; ed. by C. McDonald and J. Weckert, pp. 99-114. Los Angeles, CA, Taylor Graham, 1991.

Weckert, J. and Ferguson, S. Ethics, reference librarians and expert systems. *Australian Library Journal*, 42, 1993, 172-181.

Weibel, S. Automated cataloging: implications for libraries and patrons. In: *Artificial Intelligence and Expert Systems: Will They Change the Library?*; ed. by F. W. Lancaster and L. C. Smith, pp. 67-80. Urbana-Champaign, University of Illinois, Graduate School of Library and Information Science, 1992.

Weibel, S. et al. Automated title page cataloging: a feasibility study. *Information Processing & Management*, 25, 1989, 187-203.

Weil, B. H. et al. Technical-abstracting fundamentals. *Journal of Chemical Documentation*, 3, 1963, 86-89, 125-136.

Weiss, P. J. The Expert Cataloging Assistant Project at the National Library of Medicine. *Information Technology and Libraries*, 13, 1994, 267-271,

Weld, D., et al., eds. The role of intelligent systems in the National Information Infrastructure. *AI Magazine*, 16(3), 1995, 45-64.

Whittaker, S. et al. SCAN: designing and evaluating user interfaces to support retrieval from speech archives. In: *SIGIR '99: Proceedings of the 22nd Annual International ACM SIGIR Conference on Research and Development in Information Retrieval*, pp. 26-34. New York, Association for Computing Machinery, 1999.

Widrow, B. et al. Neural networks: applications in industry, business and science. *Communications of the ACM*, 37(3), 1994, 93-105.

Wilks, Y. et al. Combining weak methods in large-scale text processing. In: *Text-Based Intelligent Systems*; ed. by P. S. Jacobs, pp. 35-58. Hillsdale, NJ, Lawrence Erlbaum, 1992.

Williams, J. SciFinder from CAS: information at the desktop for scientists. *Online*, 19(4), 1995, 60-66.

Witbrock, M. J. and Hauptmann, A. G. Speech recognition for a digital video library. *Journal of the American Society for Information Science*, 49, 1998, 619-632.

Woelfel, J. Artificial neural networks in policy research: a current assessment. *Journal of Communication*, 43(1), 1993, 63-80.

Woodward, J. Cataloging and classifying information resources on the Internet. *Annual Review of Information Science and Technology*, 31, 1996, 189-220.

Wright, L. W. et al. Hierarchical concept indexing of full-text documents in the Unified Medical Language System information sources. *Journal of the American Society for Information Science*, 50, 1999, 514-523.

Wu, J. K. et al. CORE: a content-based retrieval engine for multimedia information systems. *Multimedia Systems*, 3, 1995, 25-41.

Xu, L. D. Developing a case-based knowledge system for AIDS prevention. *Expert Systems*, 11(4), 1994, 237-244.

Yang, Y. and Liu, X. A re-examination of text categorization methods. In: SIGIR '99 *Proceedings of the 22nd Annual International ACM SIGIR Conference on Research and Development in Information Retrieval*, pp. 42-49. New York, Association for Computing Machinery, 1999.

Young, S. J. and Chase, L. L. Speech recognition evaluation: a review of the U.S. CSR and LVCSR programmes. *Computer Speech and Language*, 12, 1998, 263-279.

Yu, H. H. and Wolf, W. A hierarchical, multi-resolution method for dictionary-driven content-based image retrieval. In: *Proceedings of the International Conference on Image Processing*, pp. 823-826. Los Alamitos, CA, IEEE, 1997.

Zager, P. and Smadi, O. A knowledge-based expert systems application in library acquisitions: monographs. *Library Acquisitions: Practice & Theory*, 16, 1992, 145-154.

Zahavi, J. and Levin, N. Issues and problems in applying neural computing to target marketing. *Journal of Direct Marketing*, 9(3), Summer 1995, 33-45.

Zahir, S. and Chang, C. K. Online-Expert: an expert system for online database selection. *Journal of the American Society for Information Science*, 43, 1992, 340-357.

Zainab, A. N. and De Silva, S. M. Expert systems in library and information services: publication trends, authorship patterns and expressiveness of published titles. *Journal of Information Science*, 24, 1998, 313-336.

Zhu, B. et al. Creating a large-scale digital library for georeferenced information. *D-Lib Magazine*, 5, 1999, http://mirrored.ukoln.ac.uk/lis-journals/dlib/dlib/july99/07zhu.html

Zhu, Q. and Stillman, M. J. Design of an expert system for emergency response to a chemical spill. *Journal of Chemical Information and Computer Sciences*, 35, 1995, 945-968.

Zizi, M. Interactive dynamic maps for visualisation and retrieval from hypertext systems. In: *Information Retrieval and Hypertext*; ed. by M. Agosti and A. F. Smeaton, pp. 203-224. Boston, Kluwer, 1996.

About the Authors

F. Wilfrid Lancaster is Professor Emeritus in the Graduate School of Library and Information Science at the University of Illinois, where he has taught courses relating to information transfer, bibliometrics, bibliographic organization, and the evaluation of library and information services. He continues to serve as editor of *Library Trends*. He was appointed University Scholar for the period 1989-1992. He is the author of eleven books, six of which have received national awards, and has three times received Fulbright fellowships for research and teaching abroad. He has received both the Award of Merit and the Outstanding Information Science Teacher award from the American Society for Information Science and Technology (ASIST). Professor Lancaster has been involved in a wide range of consulting activities, including service for UNESCO and other agencies of the United Nations.

Amy J. Warner, Ph.D. is currently a Thesaurus Design Specialist at Argus Associates, Inc. in Ann Arbor, Michigan. She was previously Associate Professor at the University of Michigan School of Information. She has more than fifteen years of experience in research and practice in information retrieval and subject access. She has participated in numerous funded studies related to the design and implementation of digital libraries, investigation of linguistic patterns in text and their implications for the design of search engines, and the understanding by end users of subject terminology. She is also co-author with F. Wilfrid Lancaster of the textbook, *Information Retrieval Today*.

INDEX

Because the entire book deals, in some way, with artificial intelligence and expert systems, these terms are not used as entry points.

More Great Books
From Information Today, Inc.

ARIST 34: Annual Review
of Information Science and Technology

Edited by Professor Martha E. Williams

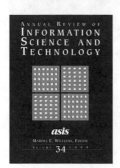

Since 1966, the *Annual Review of Information Science and Technology (ARIST)* has been continuously at the cutting edge in contributing a useful and comprehensive view of the broad field of information science and technology. ARIST reviews numerous topics within the field and ultimately provides this annual source of ideas, trends, and references to the literature. Published by Information Today, Inc. on behalf of the American Society for Information Science (ASIS), ARIST Volume 34 (1999) is the latest volume in this legendary series. The newest edition of ARIST covers the following topics:

• The History of Documentation and Information Science (Colin Burke) • Applications of Machine Learning in Information Retrieval (Sally Jo Cunningham, Jamie Littin, and Ian Witten) • Privacy and Digital Information (Philip Doty) • Cognitive Information Retrieval (Peter Ingwersen) • Text Mining (Walter Trybula) • Methodologies for Human Behavioral Research (Peiling Wang) • Measuring the Internet (Robert Williams and Bob Molyneux) • Infometric Laws (Concepcion Wilson and William Hood) • Using and Reading Scholarly Literature (Donald W. King and Carol Tenopir) • Literature Dynamics: Studies on Growth, Diffusion, and Epidemics (Albert Tabah).

Hardbound • ISBN 1-57387-093-5

ASIST Members $79.95   **Non-Members $99.95**

Introductory Concepts in Information Science

Melanie J. Norton

Melanie J. Norton presents a unique introduction to the practical and theoretical concepts of information science while examining the impact of the Information Age on society. Drawing on recent research into the field, as well as from scholarly and trade publications, the monograph provides a brief history of information science and coverage of key topics, including communications and cognition, information retrieval, bibliometrics, modeling, economics, information policies, and the impact of information technology on modern management. This is an essential volume for graduate students, practitioners, and any professional who needs a solid grounding in the field of information science.

Hardbound • ISBN 1-57387-087-0

ASIST Members $31.60   **Non-Members $39.50**

The Web of Knowledge:
A Festschrift in Honor of Eugene Garfield

Edited by Blaise Cronin and Helen Barsky Atkins

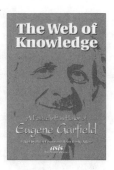

Dr. Eugene Garfield, the founder of the Institute for Scientific Information (ISI), has devoted his life to the creation and development of the multidisciplinary Science Citation Index. The index, a unique resource for scientists, scholars, and researchers in virtually every field of intellectual endeavor, has been the foundation for a multidisciplinary research community. This new ASIST monograph is the first to comprehensively address the history, theory, and practical applications of the Science Citation Index and to examine its impact on scholarly and scientific research 40 years after its inception. In bringing together the analyses, insights, and reflections of more than 35 leading lights, editors Cronin and Atkins have produced both a comprehensive survey of citation indexing and analysis and a beautifully realized tribute to Eugene Garfield and his vision.

Hardbound • ISBN 1-57387-099-4

ASIST Members $39.60   **Non-Members $49.50**

Knowledge Management
for the Information Professional

Edited by T. Kanti Srikantaiah and Michael Koenig

Written from the perspective of the information community, this book examines the business community's recent enthusiasm for Knowledge Management (KM). With contributions from 26 leading KM practitioners, academicians, and information professionals, editors Srikantaiah and Koenig bridge the gap between two distinct perspectives, equipping information professionals with the tools to make a broader and more effective contribution in developing KM systems and creating a Knowledge Management culture within their organizations.

Hardbound • ISBN 1-57387-079-X

ASIST Members $35.60   **Non-Members $44.50**

Electronic Styles
A Handbook for Citing Electronic Information

Xia Li and Nancy Crane

The second edition of the best-selling guide to referencing electronic information and citing the complete range of electronic formats includes text-based information, electronic journals and discussion lists, Web sites, CD-ROM and multimedia products, and commercial online documents.

Softbound • ISBN 1-57387-027-7 • $19.99